"Jesus, from the very beginning, has been 'good news for women.' Perhaps that news has rarely been needed more clearly than in our day. One reads of His encounters with the women described in this book with a sense of wonder that these interactions took place two thousand years ago. He is good news for women still."

—**John Ortberg**, pastor; author of *Who Is This Man?*

"What a treasure this diary-style book is! This impactful message focuses on five broken women in the Bible and their life-changing encounters with Jesus. The way Mary and Frank portray their stories will help any woman who has experienced heartbreak, loneliness, and rejection step right into the extravagant grace and love of Jesus."

—**Lysa TerKeurst**, *New York Times* bestselling author of *The Best Yes*; president of Proverbs 31 Ministries

"Mary and Frank provide a fresh look at biblical women that breathes life, color, and hue into these familiar stories. If you want to better understand the richness of biblical accounts in the context of first-century history, this is a book you won't want to miss."

—**Margaret Feinberg**, author of *Fight Back with Joy* and *Wonderstruck*

"*The Day I Met Jesus* is a refreshing look at five women in the Gospels, telling their stories in a way that brings them to life but at the same time based on careful research into the real world in which they lived. I thoroughly enjoyed this book and could not put it down. Through the eyes of women whose lives Jesus touched, this book invites us to see Jesus more deeply. It ministered to broken places in my own heart."

—**Craig Keener**, professor of New Testament, Asbury Theological Seminary

"Step into the first century, as your senses and imagination are engaged in Mary DeMuth's masterful biblical narrative, deftly exploring the hearts and minds of five women who met the Savior. Then Frank Viola brings his own gifts to the page, opening the Scriptures to help us understand each account more fully. Together, their voices sing of the beauty of Christ and the redemption He offers. *The Day I Met Jesus* is truly a wonderful book."

—**Liz Curtis Higgs**, bestselling author
of *Bad Girls of the Bible*

"We all long to lift the veil of history and catch a glimpse of the real story—the one that makes our hearts pound, our faith grow, and our lives change. That's exactly what Frank Viola and Mary DeMuth offer in this compelling book. You will never look at Scripture or God's work in your own heart the same way again after you close the final page."

—**Holley Gerth**, author of *You're Already Amazing*
and *You're Made for a God-Sized Dream*

"Elegant, stimulating, rewarding, this probe into Jesus' relationship with women packages the best of biblical scholarship and theology in the spellbinding wraps of storytelling."

—**Leonard Sweet**, bestselling author;
professor (Drew University, George Fox University);
chief contributor to Sermons.com

"Story. History. His-Story. This book has all of these and immediately gripped my heart. I held my breath as I read about women who encountered Jesus in their day. I absolutely love books that compel me to love Jesus more. Together, Frank Viola and Mary DeMuth created a masterful biblical narrative that reminds us once again how

Jesus feels about the sinner who desperately needs saving. He loves us. He came to save us. Enjoy every page of this book. You'll be glad you did."

—**Susie Larson,** radio host; national speaker; author of *Your Beautiful Purpose*

"Many Christians fail to experience the full power of the Bible's stories because they never learned how to imaginatively 'get inside' the lives of biblical characters to make them come alive. I don't know of any book that better helps readers do this than *The Day I Met Jesus*. Combining imaginative creativity, historical scholarship, and great storytelling, Viola and DeMuth help readers enter into the lives of five women in the Gospels to experience Jesus from their perspective. And by this means, they help readers deepen their own understanding of, and love for, Jesus. After reading this poignant and gripping book, you won't view these five women, Jesus, or yourself the same way!"

—**Greg Boyd**, pastor; author of *Benefit of the Doubt*, *Present Perfect*, and *The Myth of a Christian Nation*

"*The Day I Met Jesus* by Frank Viola and Mary DeMuth is destined to be a classic. Five exquisitely imaginative stories of women from the Gospels describe lives turned upside down by their encounters with Jesus. The book reveals the beauty of our Savior—His character, His compassion, His humility, His humanity, and His divinity. This gem of a book will move you, inspire you, and very likely, set you free."

—**Felicity Dale**, blogger; author of *The Black Swan Effect: A Response to Gender Hierarchy in the Church*

"In *The Day I Met Jesus*, Frank and Mary demonstrate lucid insight into the balanced, candid, focused, tender, and penetrating manner of our Master—Jesus the Christ.

See again the Savior who was God and Man embodied to show and transform us by His unpretentious holiness, empowering authenticity—without scorn or condemnation, transmitting love's purity, life's vitality, and hope's eternity. I commend the authors and this book to you: both will enrich and enlarge your thoughts and your life."

—**Pastor Jack W. Hayford**, founder
of The King's University

"The women you've always read about. Now, in real life. This fresh new take on timeless stories of the Bible's fiercest heroines will leave you inspired, empowered, and thrilled for more. Thank you, DeMuth and Viola, for this gift to women everywhere."

—**Claire Díaz-Ortiz**, Silicon Valley innovator; author;
blogger at ClaireDiazOrtiz.com

"*The Day I Met Jesus* bears the souls of five familiar women from Scripture and the deep significance of their personal encounters with Jesus. Frank Viola and Mary DeMuth have crafted a beautiful account of these women's stories with a rawness that punctuates the significance of our Savior's grace. May we be so moved to experience the love, joy, hope, and grace of the Jesus portrayed in these pages."

—**Jenni Catron**, church leader; author of *CLOUT:
Discover and Unleash Your God-Given Influence*

"Through the stories of five unique women from the Gospels, Frank Viola and Mary DeMuth masterfully reveal the truth of Jesus in a riveting, breathtaking way. Each story captivatingly invites you on a journey through pain, rejection, and brokenness and leads you right into the heart of Jesus as He meets each woman in an intimately restorative and loving way, as only Jesus can. This book will minister to the broken places in your heart and leave you longing to know Jesus more deeply."

—**Derwin L. Gray**, lead pastor of Transformation
Church; author of *Limitless Life: You Are More Than
Your Past When God Holds Your Future*

"For each of us, the day we met Jesus is to be celebrated, held in awe, memorized, and memorialized. In *The Day I Met Jesus*, Frank and Mary have enabled us to do just that alongside five women of biblical fame. Their stories are beautifully framed, permitting us to know them and walk beside them as they meet this Man and are forgiven, set free, transformed by His love and grace. And then we are taken deep into the Scriptures and our own hearts to see how Jesus wants to forgive us and set us free and, yes, transform us. You will want to read this book."

—**Judy Douglass**, author of *Letters to My Children:
Secrets of Success*; wife and partner
of Steve Douglass, President of Cru

"Everyone loves an amazing true-life story: one kissed with hope and redemption and love. *The Day I Met Jesus* is a book of such things. Smartly written and personally inspiring, Viola and DeMuth hit the mark on the beautiful lives of broken women who met the God who changed everything. Their powerful stories, written from a first-person perspective, remind me of my own brokenness and the God who rescued me too. I am grateful for this book, and I am moved."

—**Lisa Whittle**, author of *{w}hole* and *I Want God*

"I thought I knew the women in these stories well, but in this beautiful book I met each one in a fresh, personal, and profound way. The life-changing grace and mercy Christ extended to these our sisters so long ago is here right now for you and for me."

—**Sheila Walsh**, author of *The Storm Inside*

"It's one thing to skim a story about women meeting Jesus; it's another one to dive deeply into their hearts. *The Day I Met Jesus* shines the light on desperate lives and Jesus' powerful intervention. These stories made me think about my own transformation by the One I love. If you want to love Jesus more, this is the book for you. Scholarly and accurate, but also tender and beckoning, it's a book you won't want to miss!"

—**Tricia Goyer**, author of 45 books, including *One Year of Amish Peace*

"Inventive, engaging, compelling, and filled with freedom, this book will help you see the wonder of our Jesus more clearly. Here is very simply the truth about Jesus and His relationship with women: He loved us. What a powerful truth for women in the world today! Jesus is always the hero of the story. Through this book, we see and know that He is the hero of our stories too."

—**Sarah Bessey**, author of *Jesus Feminist*

THE DAY I MET
JESUS

THE DAY I MET
JESUS

The Revealing Diaries of
Five Women from the Gospels

FRANK VIOLA *and* MARY DEMUTH

BakerBooks

a division of Baker Publishing Group
Grand Rapids, Michigan

Published by Baker Books
a division of Baker Publishing Group
P.O. Box 6287, Grand Rapids, MI 49516-6287
www.bakerbooks.com

Printed in the United States of America

Library of Congress Cataloging-in-Publication Data is on file at the Library of Congress, Washington, DC.

ISBN 978-0-8010-1685-1 (pbk.)

Published in association with the literary agency of The Fedd Agency, Inc., Austin, TX.

Published in association with the literary agency of Daniel Literary Group, LLC, Nashville, TN.

15 16 17 18 19 20 21   8 7 6 5 4 3 2

Contents

Jesus Christ is the same yesterday, today,
and forever.

—Hebrews 13:8 NLT

Why We Wrote This Book

PREFACE BY FRANK VIOLA

In 2013, I released my first work of biblical narrative. *God's Favorite Place on Earth* told the story of Jesus and His frequent visits to the little village of Bethany as told through the eyes of Lazarus.

As I wrote *God's Favorite Place on Earth*, I had it on my heart to follow it up with another book that tells the story of five specific women in the Gospels and their remarkable encounters with the Lord Jesus.

I didn't feel comfortable writing from the viewpoint of a woman, so I asked the most gifted Christian fiction writer of our time—Mary DeMuth—to coauthor the book.

Given how prolific Mary is, I was honored she accepted my request.

In this book Mary and I tell the story of five different women who met Jesus and the incredible effect He had on each of their lives.

We have filled in the details of each Gospel story by creating dialogue, action, and atmosphere. These details add color and texture to the narratives. We have drawn these creative details from first-century history so they are consistent with the biblical record and New Testament scholarship.

Like *God's Favorite Place on Earth*, this isn't a scholarly work. Different possibilities derived from the biblical data are deliberately left out. Our narration is according to what we consider to be the best research available today.

In the pages that follow, you will hear each woman tell her story in her own words. Following each narrative is a "Walking It Out" section that practically applies the crucial points of each narrative to our lives today. The book concludes with a "Talking It Over" section to help churches and small groups navigate the content.

As you hear each woman write about her life-changing encounter with the Son of God, we expect the profound significance of how Jesus interacted with them to turn your own world upside down just as it did theirs.

Frank Viola
May 2014

Preface by Mary DeMuth

When Frank approached me about partnering with him, I was intrigued. I have a heart for women in desperate situations. I've been one, and I've seen Jesus intersect my anguish with outlandishly surprising love. As a storyteller, I loved the challenge of getting to know these five women and giving them flesh, bones, emotions, guts, and authenticity.

In the process of writing their stories, I found further freedom.

We wrote this book because we want to see Jesus set you free. We want you to approach His enormous throne of grace with complete confidence—the throne of a King who dared to wear human skin, to welcome outcasts, and to grant deep dignity to those on the fringes of this world.

By telling the story of five desperate women found in the Gospels, we are telling your story, our story, the world's story—the story of a people longing to be validated, heard, and commissioned, no matter what the circumstance.

If you are lonely, you will find Jesus in these pages.

If you are broken, expect to find wholeness.

If you are living on the outskirts of life, Jesus welcomes you back in.

If you have lost hope, you will recapture it through the words and actions of your glorious Lord.

If you have given up on Christianity, you'll learn the true nature of Christ—how beautifully He gives Himself to the powerless.

We expect all of these things to happen to you as you hear five stories from the hearts of the women themselves who had incredible encounters with Jesus Christ.[1] We have woven the history, culture, and ancient social setting into their stories so you can experience Jesus as they did.

You will encounter the Lord in surprising new ways as you meet Him through . . .

The woman caught in the act of adultery.

The woman who loved too much.

The woman longing for eternal water.

The woman who bled and bled and bled.

The woman who audaciously sat at Jesus' feet.

Dare to place yourself in the footsteps of these women whose lives were changed forever by Jesus Christ, and be ready for your life to be wholly changed as well.

Mary DeMuth
May 2014

Introducing
Five Amazing Encounters

> Then the two from Emmaus told their story of how Jesus
> had appeared to them as they were walking along the
> road, and how they had recognized him as he was break-
> ing the bread.
>
> —Luke 24:35 NLT

In Luke 24, the author tells an incredible story about the risen Christ. It goes something like this.

It's a Sunday evening in AD 30. Earlier that morning the greatest historical event known to humankind occurred: *Jesus of Nazareth rose from the dead*.

As the sun begins to set, two disciples of Jesus walk from Jerusalem to the town of Emmaus. They are husband and wife. Cleopas and his wife Mary.[1]

This couple has been following Jesus for a number of years. Perplexed and saddened, they had expected Jesus to save Israel from pagan domination. But instead, the Romans put the young prophet to death in the most violent way. Hanging from a cross with the blood of God and man dripping to the earth. A crown of thorns replaced what should have been a crown of imperial glory.

As Cleopas and Mary walk along the road to Emmaus, a mysterious stranger joins them. The stranger inquires about their conversation. They respond, "We followed a prophet who we thought was the Messiah. We hoped that He was the One who would redeem Israel. But He can't be the Messiah because He was put to death on a cross."

This mysterious stranger is Jesus, the risen Lord. But they do not recognize Him.

Fully aware that they do not know who He is, Jesus strikes up a conversation with the couple, and in so doing He reframes the entire Old Testament story. He doesn't deviate from the scriptural narrative, but He tells the story anew and afresh. He adds Technicolor to the black-and-white way they had heard the story all their lives.

Jesus essentially says, "You've not understood the story correctly. You've been reading your Bible through the wrong end of the lens."[2]

Opened Eyes and Burning Hearts

So beginning with Moses and all the Prophets, Jesus retells the narrative. As He unfolds the story, the "why" of Jesus' death suddenly dawns on them and their hearts begin to burn.

Still captivated, Mary and Cleopas invite this intriguing stranger for dinner, and He accepts.

As He reclines at table, the Lord breaks bread, blesses it, and passes it on to them. Immediately, their eyes are opened. They recognize this stranger is no stranger at all. It is the risen Christ, Jesus of Nazareth, the One whom they have been following all along.

Luke writes, "Their eyes were opened and they knew."

This sentence echoes Genesis 3, when another couple ate a different kind of food and "their eyes were opened and they knew."[3]

The message is clear: In His resurrection, the Lord Jesus Christ has reversed the fall of man and ushered in a new creation. What once seemed lost is now found. That which is broken beyond repair is restored to life. Dead dreams became resurrected hope—all because of Jesus' raucous resurrection.

Encountering Jesus Today

Fast-forward to the present.

The world is full of people who walk to and fro, disappointed, disheartened, and perplexed.

Most Westerners have heard a diluted version of the gospel. In fact, they have heard the story incorrectly. The biblical story has been stripped, added to, and complicated. For countless Christians, the story of Scripture has become all too familiar. It lacks color, redemption, and life.

The need of the hour, then, is to tell the story differently . . .

To tell it differently to those who don't know Jesus.

To tell it differently to the broken and downcast.

To tell it differently to the church.

To tell it differently to one another.

Out of His infinite mercy, we both have experienced Jesus on the road to Emmaus, and it has caused us to exclaim a holy "aha" as we have encountered His outrageous love.

Jesus is a beautiful Revolutionary—not overturning governments, but conquering hearts and making them burn with joy.

The Austrian philosopher Ivan Illich said it best when he wrote, "Neither revolution nor reformation can ultimately change a society, rather you must tell a new powerful tale, one so persuasive that it sweeps away the old myths and becomes the preferred story. . . . If you want to change a society, then you have to tell an alternative story."

We hope this little book ushers in that kind of change in your heart, your home, and your life.

1

Diary of a Woman Caught in Adultery

I wanted to keep my story to myself, cradle it like a mother caresses a baby in the secret place of the night, but today I remembered that some stories cry their way to the streets. I must have become brazen, or far too graced in the months following my encounter. Because I dared to approach the temple in search of something. Someone.

Jesus, the One who liberated me from shame, met His demise at the hands of both Jew and Roman. Rumors now flew of Him walking the streets of this earth. A ghost perhaps? A wishful hope? After all, many men resembled the simple carpenter from Nazareth. The hope I nurtured felt ragged, and yet the hand of God compelled me to the street today, winding through dusty roads, until I could almost taste the sacrifices on my tongue. As I paced back and forth, afraid to mount the hill leading to the place of worship, I rehashed the story in my mind with each step I took.

That story began with a man, and it ended with a Man. But oh the difference in between the two. One stole my life; the other offered it back.

Eleazar had struck me across the face that morning. I felt the sting on my cheek through most of the day.

"You whorish dog!" he yelled. Loud enough for my boy, Jotham, to hear. Jotham scampered away, trying to hide in the darkened corner of our small home. If only I could make myself that small, that inconspicuous.

I readied myself for the inevitable second blow. I prayed. *Dear God, Lord of heaven's great armies, do You see me here? Alone except for Jotham whom I desperately want to protect. As Hagar named You El Roi, the God who sees, I cry out to You. I am Hagar today. Unloved. Despairing. She is me. I am her, except that I am bereaved of Your presence.*

Eleazar loomed above me, a sneer decorating his face. He held up the earthen pot containing the morning's breakfast I had scalded. Cooking is still a mystery to me.

"I have had enough of your careless ways, your utter disregard for my family, my son, my home. You are trash! You will pay, and the payment will be swift." With that he threw the pot on the earthen floor. And it shattered across the house. I sheltered Jotham from its shards.

Eleazar laughed until his voice reverberated the walls. He struck me again in the same place. I sunk to the ground, holding my jaw, counting my teeth with my tongue. As quickly as he hit me, he left. When he exited, I let out my breath. Had I been holding it for hours? As I gathered up the broken pottery, I realized I was like those shards of earthenware—shattered, broken at inconceivable angles, never to be remade.

I looked at my dear son. His eyes were wide and he breathed heavy. "Why can we not leave him, Mama? He will kill you someday."

"We would be destitute, son," I told him. "No food nor shelter. And no way to make a living. The world does not look kindly upon women who leave their husbands. Besides, he would demand you stay within his care. And I cannot let that happen." I pulled Jotham close to myself, kissed his tousled head. *Oh dear God in heaven, I love this child.*

I hurried outside to ensure Eleazar had left. I could see him far down the pathway, speaking to Shechem, the merchant of stunning cloth who befriended me several Sabbaths ago. Eleazar's arms gesticulated, rage-filled, and I imaged the conversation. "You cannot talk to my wife. You cannot help her, and you cannot befriend her. She is to be isolated for her insolence."

Those were the only words he could be saying, so I sunk back into our small home, wiping away tears. Not even Shechem could rescue me.

"Why are you crying, Mama?"

I touched Jotham's sweet boy cheek. "It is the dust of the day kicking up again. Do not worry." I wiped my eyes to show him, but I knew he understood my lies. He had seen so many tears in six years of life.

When my father had told me of Eleazar, my heart leapt. I did not know him as a friend. We did not grow up in the same village or run in packs as children do before they attend synagogue. But I had heard whispers about him from my friends—whispers of his stature, his charm, his intelligence, and his handsome face. And when I spied him after my father told me he chose Eleazar to be my husband, I smiled.

Ours would not be a marriage of two families as much as it would be a union of love.

And it was. For a time. Until Jotham cried his way into the world, bright-eyed and lung-strong. Eleazar's feelings shifted with the birth of our boy. I could see in the way he dismissed me that his great affection changed from loving me to holding this tiny namesake in his arms.

Odd, now in retrospect, as Eleazar does not take care of Jotham and does not teach him as a rabbi would gently lead a learner, does not swing him around on lanky limbs, does not tell him funny stories or pray for him after sundown.

No, he likes the *idea* of Jotham. He is happy to have offspring—a boy to carry on his family name. Had I birthed a girl, would he have loved me longer—in anticipation of an heir?

I gave Jotham some porridge I had hidden. My stomach rumbled.

"You have some too, Mother."

"No, I have already eaten. It is for you."

Jotham angled me an I-do-not-believe-you look, but ate the small amount anyway. He then grabbed his satchel and ran toward the House of the Book, our local synagogue, where he had been learning for one year now. Such a smart, smart child.

"I love you," I said. But the Judean wind stole my words away. I sat hard on the dirt floor, cupping my face in my hands, telling myself to breathe, to feel, to live. Eleazar had stolen so much of me. I used to laugh. I once dreamed of making garments for princes and elders and dignitaries. My skills brought me praise in the market, and Shechem's fabric made my tunics sing. This one thing brought small shreds of joy, only to have each denarius grabbed from my hand and placed in Eleazar's purse. At least I could revel in my creations. At least that mended my heart a little.

A noise at our home's entrance shuddered me. I looked up and then stood.

Shechem loomed there, broad shouldered, eyes smiling.

I thought of my neighbors, how their tongues would wag at this visitor. I looked around, seeing no one, which both excited and unnerved me. Where was everyone?

I wiped my face of tears, hoping he had not seen my vulnerability. "But my husband," I said. "Just now I saw him talking to you."

"He says a great many things," Shechem said. "But I am a man with my own mind. I do not believe everything I hear." He held up some breathtaking cloth, cobalt blue with pearly white swirls. "You like this?"

"But if he sees the tunics I create from your cloth, he will hurt me. I saw how he stood furious near you."

"He will not know. You simply tell him you found another cloth merchant. It is really quite simple." He moved toward me.

I stepped back, nerves tingling through me. Shechem had been so caring, so alert to my needs, to my story. And yet . . .

He touched my cheek, the very place where Eleazar had bruised me.

I pulled away. "No."

He backed away, arms in the air. "Forgive me," he said. "It is your beauty that compelled me."

Beauty? When had Eleazar called me beautiful? I could not remember such a time. I shook my head. "I am married. I may be unhappy, but I am an honorable woman."

"So you are. A beautiful treasure of a woman." He noticed something on the floor, picked it up—a shard from the broken vessel. "Did he throw this at you?"

"He did not." I answered honestly. "He threw it at the floor in anger. I burned the morning meal. I displeased him. So in a way, you could say it was my fault the pot broke." My familiar friend, shame, slithered through me.

Like the vessel, I deserved to be broken. If only I could perform everything perfectly, to Eleazar's standards. If I never burned the meals. If I always responded affectionately to his demanding advances. If I parented Jotham correctly so he never acted up. If the home stayed as clean as Solomon's palace. If. If. If.

Shechem moved toward me. Held my chin gently. I did not retreat this time, though everything inside told me to run. I am Bathsheba bathing on the rooftops, and the king has sent for me. I feel helpless to resist. My loneliness and inward emptiness hold me to the ground, stifling my will to push back.

"You deserve better. You are as Queen Esther, a woman of valor."

"I am nothing of the sort."

"Come with me. I have a hidden place where we can be alone. No one will see us. It will be our secret. Eleazar will not find out. The world will never know."

"But God will know. I will know." My words sounded entirely small. Helpless words. He slid his arm behind me and pulled me near. I could smell his breath, his sweat. What had God done for me? Why had He not heard my thousand cries of desperation? Why had I been slotted for such a life? All these thoughts coursed through me as I lay my head on Shechem's shoulder and felt his heart beat through his tunic. To feel his arms around me, to understand tenderness, to be beautifully loved. Is not this what I had asked the Almighty for these six years?

I looked into Shechem's brown eyes and allowed him to drink in mine. A small voice inside me screamed, *run, run, run*, but Shechem's draw felt irresistible. Flashes of our childhood friendship flittered through my mind. The kindness. The compliments. How he asked me questions. The many times he praised my work. So unlike Eleazar.

My mind hazed as my desire bloomed in his embrace.

"Come with me," he said.

I looked around for my neighbors, still no other women. The cry in my heart to be cherished silenced my dying conscience. I had to push Jotham from my mind, but before I could, I envisioned him safe with my parents, safely away from his father. Yes, my son would be safe there.

"I cannot," I told him. "Others will see."

He winked at me. "I talked to your neighbors first," he said. "I told them that the teacher Jesus was near, and that if they hurried, they could see Him. We are alone. But they will return, so we must be quick."

I did not answer. Shechem took my hand in his. I followed him, sealing my fate. I would be loved. One last time.

At the doorway of a home I had never been to, Shechem lifted me into his arms and carried me effortlessly into its entrance. He set me down, put his hands on my shoulders, and held my eyes with his. He kissed me, then, long and hungry. And for what seemed like eternity, I kissed him back, giving in to his desires, my desires. We nearly became one flesh.

But then a vision of Jotham's face stopped my forbidden thoughts cold. I backed away, bile choking my throat. I coughed. "My son," I said. "What will happen to my son?"

But Shechem did not answer. Instead he pulled me again to himself and kissed me, his beard burning my face and the force of his grip aching the cheek Eleazar had recently struck.

"Please, Shechem. If you love me—"

"I know how to prove my love to a beautiful woman like you," he said. He backed away. "You are free to go," he said, "but we will not always have this chance."

I could remedy this decision, even now. I could leave this place, run far away from this man, and we would continue on as if nothing happened. This is what I wanted. Adultery carried a stoning penalty. I turned to leave.

"Do not leave," he said. Not as demand, but as pleading. Tears streaked his face, gathering in his beard. "I love you," he said.

And with those three words, I let go of everything sacred— my vow to God to be a chaste and respectful woman, the covenant I made with my husband to love him only, the consequences my actions would have on my son.

We did become one.

And once we did, I felt ill.

Shechem gazed at me, a smile playing on his lips. "Worth the chase," he said. "Especially after I receive payment."

"What?"

He stood, now looming over my half-clothed body. "She is here, and I am finished with her."

Three religious leaders from my synagogue stepped into the room after Shechem stepped away. He secured his tunic, but I lay there half naked. I wondered if they would do what Shechem had done, but they did not. My heartbeat counted to three hundred as the world stopped spinning. They leered.

I shivered.

I gathered my clothes, pulling my tunic around me, but I still felt exposed. One man, one, I think his name was Benjamin, grabbed my arm and pulled me heavenward. "You will stay as you are, Adulteress. No time to cover yourself as you would like. Besides," he told another man, "her disheveled state will better prove our case."

I had no name now. Very little covering. No dignity. Instead what I wore was red-faced shame and utter terror.

Shechem slipped away. The three men manhandled me and dragged me outside. I could sense their glee and triumph.

"Now what will Jesus of Nazareth say to this," Benjamin sneered.

The other two laughed, then each man spat on me. I prayed their spittle would become a shield about me, as God promised King David. Had he not violated the laws of God too? And yet God had mercy on him. Had I not been a woman after the Almighty's heart? But even as I prayed, the noonday sun pierced through me as we left the shelter of narrow roads and houses that shaded my walk of shame into the broad upward pathway toward the temple. I had tried to cover my head, but Benjamin grabbed the cloth from me.

Dear God, no.

I dug in my heels as rocks pierced my feet. "No," I said.

But they did not listen. They continued to drag me, hurling insults as they did.

"He paid us well, and we have been amply rewarded," Benjamin said. "We will now see what the false teacher has to say about her."

The other two laughed. One said, "Discovering an adulteress in the act is never an easy task."

Who paid them? Shechem? Eleazar?

I looked down at my half-covered body, aware of the stares of children from behind mothers' dresses, widows clucking their judgment, gossip-women wild with fury over my offense. I felt the weight of some men's lust-laden looks. I was dead now. I had a growing sense that I would never, ever live again. "He will finally have to answer for His loose interpretations of the Law." Benjamin yanked my arm. I cried out. "You, little adulteress, will be the trap we need."

"What do you mean?" I asked.

But he hit me across the same swollen cheek. I held my silence, then.

The three men hurled me at the feet of a Rabbi who must have been teaching because a crowd had gathered before Him. I could not lift my eyes, or look up at the crowd. I told myself not to shake, but the shivering continued even as the sun beat upon me.

"Teacher," Benjamin said to Jesus, "this woman was caught in the act of adultery. The Law of Moses says to stone her."

Oh dear God. I will die soon, abandoning my precious son to this cruel world. And I walked willingly to Shechem's lair. I kissed him. I said yes. I deserved this death. But that deserving did nothing to stop my trembling.

A group of men surrounded me. I would not pick my head up to see the stones in their hands. Head down, I could see only their sandals through my tears.

One of them yelled to the Rabbi, "Moses commands us to stone her! What do you say?"

I expected words from this man.

But He stood mute.

I dared to lift my eyes slightly a hesitant moment, only to see this work-worn man stoop to earth and draw in the dust with His finger. What did He draw? Something about this man brought peace to the heartbeat that had lodged in my throat. How He stooped. How He did not give in to the demands of these leaders.

Shouts from the crowd echoed through me. "Stone her! Stone her! Stone her!" I ducked my head and waited for the rocks to crush me.

Benjamin nearly growled his words. "Rabbi, we demand an answer!"

The once-hunched Rabbi sat up straight, and it was then He looked at me. His eyes. Oh dear Lord, His eyes. They saw me. In that hiccup of glances, I somehow knew that He discerned my day, my story, my heart. He knew my entrapment and abduction. Would He shield . . . ?

He looked at the three men, and as He did, the crowd who yelled *stone her* quieted.

He straightened Himself and uttered these simple words: "Let the one who has never sinned throw the first stone!"

A long pause followed.

Never sinned?

Shame flooded through me. I could not answer for those who wanted to throw stones or even for the Pharisees who had dragged me here, but I knew myself. I had sinned. Great and small. In thought and deed. If this be true (and I knew it was), at least I could not cast a stone at myself. He made it very clear—only a sinless person wielded the power of life and death.

From where I lay crumpled, I dared not look up. With head down, I squinted through my tears. A sea of sandaled feet populated the horizon. They did not move, tethered to the earth. The men whose feet these were would soon throw heavy stones to crush the life out of me. I trembled, waiting for the first stone to hit my head.

I heard the sound of stones falling to the ground one by one. *Thud.* Pause. *Thud, thud.*

I watched, through tear-stained eyes, as each stone created a dust whirl in the heat of day.

What happened? I coughed. Then tasted copper on my tongue as if I had finally come to my senses—my blood.

I stole a glance to my left and noticed a set of sandaled feet disappear. Then another. Then ten others, one by one. I snuck a peek around me as the circle wanting vengeance widened, stones now marking the place where my accusers once stood.

The Rabbi stooped to earth again and drew in the sand.

I dropped my head, then dared to look up again. I only saw one more set of sandals to my right. Shortly, those sandals also disappeared.

Only two of us stood in what was once my circle of accusers. The soft-spoken Rabbi, who still scribbled in the dust, and me—a woman caught in the act of adultery.

The wind stilled. The rocks stood like sentries around us, tokens of what could have meant my violent death. Would I be Goliath, as David slung a well-aimed rock at my forehead? Would this Rabbi gather stones from the dust and take my life?

The Rabbi sat up again and asked, "Where are your accusers? Did not even one of them condemn you?"

"No, Lord," I said. For this man was no mere man.

He took the blue and white fabric at my feet and covered me. As He did, the blood in my mouth evaporated in an instant. He touched my cheek where Eleazar had struck, Shechem gripped, and Benjamin hit. The pain ceased. He gently touched my shoulders, and as He did, I sensed that God had indeed answered every prayer I had ever prayed. He had heard my cries of desperation and worry and fear. He was utterly mindful of my lot in life. And He cared. Deeply.

In that circle of two, the entire world fell away. My accusers melted into the Judean sun. My fears sloughed from me in a beautiful redemption.

The Rabbi said, "Neither do I condemn you. Go and sin no more."

I left the temple area a different woman. A loved woman like Bathsheba. A seen woman like Hagar. A queen like Esther. I had been exposed and accused, yet I had escaped the wrath of both man and God. That kind of grace changed me utterly.

That was the day Jesus of Nazareth saw me. And loved me.

In the months following I did not reconcile with Eleazar. He issued a divorce decree, said he did not want Jotham. A gift from the Almighty.

I healed in heart and soul and continued my work with cloth, until Jotham ran to me breathless one Friday. "They are crucifying Jesus," he wailed.

We ran all the way, me tugging at his arm, he trying desperately to match my stride, until we reached the Place of the Skull where three rudimentary crosses jutted from the earth. The ground beneath us smelled of urine, and I briefly worried for Jotham's health. But I could not pull my gaze away from the crosses. Flanked by two criminals (they both had been notorious thieves), Jesus awkwardly stood, knees bent, a thorny crown jutting into His skull. Blood ran red from His head, His wrists, His ankles.

Utterly alone, Jesus labored to breathe, pulling Himself up on the spikes to drag in another cupful of air, only to relapse to bended knees and suffocation. This crucifixion was a barbaric practice, I knew. I covered Jotham's eyes with my tunic, turned him toward me to keep away the horror.

Angry men hurled insults and accusations, though He did nothing to deserve such torment, such untruth. I knew He must have been dragged and beaten and harassed in the same manner as myself, yet He kept his protests to Himself, did not defend Himself.

I could not shout "He who is without sin, crucify this man!" because I feared the crowds. But I felt those words. This man, this Jesus, had no sin—I knew that like

I understood a mother's love for a son. And yet I watched as He chose to endure the cross of His own volition. For me. For them. For this broken world.

In a way He took up stones and threw them at Himself.

Even in agony, even as guards cast lots for his bloodied clothing, He pulled to stand, to drag in another breath and say, "Father, forgive them, for they do not know what they are doing." Even then, forgiveness bled from Jesus' mouth. He uttered those words not just for those who jeered and wagged their heads, but for all of us who walked this dusty place called earth, who desperately needed to know that no sin could ever, ever separate us from an extraordinary, loving, sacrificing God.

A God who goes to such lengths as to stand up to the religiously pious and die for all who wore the garment of sin. Their sin—my sin—became the rocks that would kill Him, though it was not stones that took His life. Crucifixion accomplished its terrible job.

He died there, alone, agonized. I felt His death through me, around me, beneath me as the ground shook angry rumbles.

I pulled the multicolored tunic around Jotham and me, both of us shivering from the darkness.

Jotham looked up at me. "Why did He have to die, Mama?"

I had no answer for him then. I could only weep at the injustice of an innocent man dying a criminal's death. And wonder why I had been spared such a fate—a woman undeserving of grace.

Weeks later, the memories of that horrid crucifixion haunted me as I finished my pilgrimage and stood outside the temple. I took note of one of the men who had dragged me to His feet on the day of my shame. He met my eyes, but I could not discern what I saw there. Hatred? Embarrassment? Shame? Anger? Indifference?

He hurried away, but I ran after him. Why? I do not know, nor can I explain what compelled me to do so. "Wait," I said.

He turned, his eyes haunted.

We stood in the exact place Jesus had told me to sin no more. I wondered if the man knew this, or if my chasing had frightened him. We looked at each other, neither speaking for a long moment. I remembered how rocks littered the circle, but not one person had hurled one my way.

The man cleared his throat. His face reddened. "He is alive," he hushed. And with those words, he turned and darted away.

Once again I stood alone in this place, the place of both shame and awakening. At my feet I noticed a rock. I picked it up, felt its weight in my hands. I brought it to my face, forgetting the dust, and kissed it. And as I did, I noticed a Man a few paces away.

Drawing in the dirt.

THE SACRED TEXT

They all went home, but Jesus went to the Mount of Olives. At dawn he appeared again in the temple courts, where all the people gathered around him, and he sat down to teach them. The teachers of the law and the Pharisees brought in a woman caught in adultery. They made her stand before the group and said to Jesus, "Teacher, this woman was caught in the act of adultery. In the Law Moses commanded us to stone such women. Now what do you say?" They were using this question as a trap, in order to have a basis for accusing him.

But Jesus bent down and started to write on the ground with his finger. When they kept on questioning him, he straightened up and said to them, "Let any one of you who is without sin be the first to throw a stone at her." Again he stooped down and wrote on the ground.

At this, those who heard began to go away one at a time, the older ones first, until only Jesus was left, with the woman still standing there. Jesus straightened up and asked her, "Woman, where are they? Has no one condemned you?"

"No one, sir," she said.

"Then neither do I condemn you," Jesus declared. "Go now and leave your life of sin."

—John 7:53–8:11

WALKING IT OUT

In many Bibles, the story you just read in John 7:53 to John 8:11 is set off in brackets. In other translations, it appears in a footnote.

Why? Because many scholars believe this portion of the text wasn't an original part of the Gospel of John. The earliest manuscripts don't have it, later manuscripts insert it in other parts of John, and some manuscripts place it in Luke.

But whether the text was an original part of John's Gospel or not, it has been held throughout church history that the story is authentic and rings true to the ministry of Jesus. So we believe, along with countless scholars past and present, that the narrative represents a real event from the life of Christ.

The Chess Match

This story opens with the scribes and Pharisees leveling a test at Jesus' feet. Jesus sat in the women's court of the temple, teaching the people.

Seeking to entrap Jesus, the scribes and Pharisees burst into the women's court and threw a married (or betrothed) woman before Him. They "caught" her in the act of adultery and seized her.

Consider the specific test they were putting forth: "Teacher, this woman has been caught in the act of adultery. Now the Law of Moses commanded us to stone such women. So what do you say?"

According to the Law of Moses, "If a man is found lying with the wife of another man, *both of them* shall die" (Deut. 22:22 ESV, emphasis added; Lev. 20:10).

Note that the Law of Moses demanded the execution of both adulterous parties (per the emphasis). Since witnesses were necessary, the sinning parties had to be caught in the act (Deut. 17:6; 19:15).

In this situation the scribes and Pharisees appear to have set this woman up. One indication is that the man is nowhere to be found. It takes two people to commit adultery, so where is he? It's possible they paid the man off, and he left the scene quietly while they dragged the woman off to the temple courts.

We know from John 8:6 that the leaders' motives were malevolent. "This they said to test him, that they might have some charge to bring against him."[1] Clearly they weren't seeking honest guidance from Jesus, they schemed to entrap Him.

This shouldn't surprise us because the scribes and Pharisees often tested Jesus throughout the Gospels (Matt. 22:25; Mark 8:11; 10:2; 12:15). This time, however, they used a woman as a pawn to try to put the Lord into checkmate. Their intention was to throw Him on the horns of a dilemma that He could not escape.

A Dilemma That Only God Can Escape

The scribes and Pharisees think they have Jesus cornered. Here's why.

If Jesus responded, "Stone her," He would be contradicting His teachings of mercy, grace, and forgiveness, proving He was just as harsh and cruel as the religious leaders. In so doing He would lose the favor of His followers who hung upon His grace-laced words.

He also could be charged with sedition before the Roman governor. While the Jewish Sanhedrin held the right to *pronounce* the sentence of capital offenses against Jewish laws, the Roman administration held the exclusive right to *execute* people for such offenses (John 18:31).

If on the other hand He said, "Do not stone her," He would be in violation of the Law of Moses.

So the scribes and Pharisees believe they have the young prophet in checkmate. Jesus was forced to either reject Jewish law (which would turn all devout Jews against Him) or reject Roman rule (which would allow the Jewish leaders to accuse Jesus before the Roman officials).[2]

Indeed, this was a trap that only God could escape.

But they underestimated the young prophet who was wiser than all of them combined. And this wisdom blended with something they did not possess: grace and mercy.

Words in the Dust

It's interesting that Jesus ignored the scribes and Pharisees' testing question. Instead, He simply stooped down and wrote in the dirt.

What did He write, exactly?

No mortal knows.

Perhaps He wrote, "I desire mercy, and not sacrifice."

Or perhaps He penned a list of sins . . . the sins of the witnesses who were reaching for stones.

Or perhaps He imitated the act of a Roman magistrate, who first wrote down his sentence before reading it out loud. (Jesus' verdict is found in John 8:7.) If this is so, He wrote His acquittal first and then perhaps "guilty" as a verdict for the accusers the second time He wrote in the dust.

Or perhaps He wrote the opening words of Exodus 23:1, "Do not help a guilty person by being a malicious witness."

Or perhaps He alluded to Jeremiah 17:13, "Those who turn away from you will be written in the dust because they have forsaken the Lord, the spring of living water."

Or perhaps He mimicked His Father, who wrote the ten commandments with His finger, etching the commandment about not coveting your neighbor's wife. A text that would render all the Jewish leaders guilty (Matt. 5:28).

Or perhaps He simply doodled, making a mockery of their question with the very contempt it deserved.

Amid the Lord's silence, the scribes and Pharisees persisted in repeating their question. The disciples probably mused, *How's He going to get out of this one?*

Checkmate

When Jesus sat up straight and replied with, "Let the one who is without sin cast the first stone," He did more than shock everyone present. Your Lord was turning the tables on His detractors, and in so doing He put a group of jealous religious elitists into checkmate.

The holy Son of God took all embarrassment away from the woman and placed her shame squarely on the shoulders of the scribes and Pharisees.

To use a different metaphor, the Lord's detractors not only lost their prey that day, but also their bait. One can't help but admire a Lord like that and be in awe at His wisdom and grace.

Jesus and Women

There's something else in this story that's often overlooked. The scribes and Pharisees chose a woman to be their example instead of a man. They could have easily entrapped a man and made him the example to put Jesus to the test. But they chose a woman, reinforcing a common mentality in that day.

The overall culture held women to a different standard than men. They were sometimes treated as scapegoats, and many took their sin more seriously than men's transgressions.

But the Lord stood against sexual stereotyping and religious scapegoating. He had a strong aversion to double standards.[3]

Throughout His ministry, Christ exalted women as equal to men. He was the only teacher of His day who had female disciples. What is more, every sin that a man committed was no different in His eyes than if a woman had committed it. And He died for all of them.

"Neither Do I Condemn You"

And now we press the question that is so rarely asked whenever this story is read.

Who is this woman?

The answer may surprise you.

She's you.

And she's us.

Perhaps you've never been caught in the physical act of adultery, per se, but we have all been "caught" in our sins. Let's not forget that Jesus called a lustful look adultery (Matt. 5:28). By the same token James said that if you break one commandment, you've broken them all (James 2:10). That places all of us, men and women alike, on the same moral level. We have all sinned.

If every Christian would have eyes to see this truth, we would humbly eliminate all self-righteousness from our hearts. In short, we are all made of clay; we all have the propensity to sin.

With one devastating statement Jesus demonstrated that the Law wasn't wrong, but if everyone saw the Law for what it was, we would understand that we are *all* guilty. Including the self-anointed, puritanical, moral guardians known as the scribes and Pharisees . . . and those who follow in their footsteps.

Greater Than Moses

It's interesting that John 8 opens with a group of men wanting to stone a woman, and it ends with a group of men wanting to stone Jesus.

When people's hypocrisy is exposed, the typical instinct is to kill the person who did the exposing. And that's exactly what Jesus did in this scene. Self-righteous men exposed an adulterous woman. A merciful prophet exposed the hypocrisy of religious leaders.

It's hypocritical for sinners to want to harm other sinners because of sin.[4] According to Jesus, only the guiltless could rightfully carry out such a righteous sentence of justice.

Unfortunately, this same judgmental attitude lives in the hearts of many self-righteous Christians today. These are those who clearly see the evil in others while being blind to the evil residing in their own hearts. Or as Philip Yancey once put it, some "Christians get very angry at those who sin differently than they do."[5]

In the mind of God, righteousness and justice are grounded in grace. Whenever grace is removed, we are left with the heartless hypocrisy of Pharisaism.

In this story, Jesus Christ didn't overturn the Law. Instead, He reestablished righteousness on the basis of grace. He essentially said to the woman, "Don't sin like this again." Not because she might be stoned. But because grace had rescued her—and she now possessed a new identity as a beautifully loved child of God.

45

Jesus is the Prophet who is greater than Moses. While the Law demanded execution, Jesus reestablished righteousness on the basis of grace.

> For the law was given through Moses; grace and truth came through Jesus Christ. (John 1:17)

> For the grace of God has appeared that offers salvation to all people. It teaches us to say "No" to ungodliness and worldly passions, and to live self-controlled, upright and godly lives in this present age. (Titus 2:11–12)

Don't misunderstand. Sin is heinous. Whether it takes the form of adultery, or slander, or abusive words in a fit of rage, or jealousy, or gossip, or lying (pick your sin), God doesn't ignore it because sin harms the people He created.

Yet a person who brings correction to those who hurt others ought to do it with no hint of self-righteousness in their hearts, knowing full well that they are equally fallen and capable of much worse (Gal. 6:1–5).

If a person is walking in the Spirit of Christ and they confront another person, they will experience more (or as much) pain as the person they are correcting. Why? Because they know how clay-footed they themselves are. And because they are humble, they realize just how precarious they themselves are in living a holy life.

Grace ushers in forgiveness, but it also empowers us to walk in a new way.

Holiness, then, is built on the experience of grace, not on the fear of the Law.

Christ came not to judge the world, but to save it (John 12:47). He's in the business of rescuing and releasing us, while at the same time calling our sin for what it is: self-centeredness.

As mere mortals, none of us has the capacity to correctly judge the human heart. Humans skim the outside, but God delves into the inside (1 Sam. 16:7). "Mercy triumphs over judgment" (James 2:13). And the way in which we judge is the way we will be judged (Matt. 7:2).

Yet only in Christ do mercy and truth shake hands. Only in Him do righteousness and truth kiss one another (Ps. 85:10).

Never forget: You have a Lord who does not accuse you (Rev. 12:10; Rom. 8:33–34). If you have received Jesus Christ as your Lord and Savior, you are set blessedly free from condemnation. Not only can you not be condemned, you can't even be indicted. Why? Because you are in Christ, and He's unindictable.

> Therefore there is now no condemnation for those who are in Christ Jesus. (Rom. 8:1 NASB)

> Who will bring any charge against those whom God has chosen? It is God who justifies. Who then is the one who condemns? No one. Christ Jesus who died—more than that, who was raised to life—is at the right hand of God and is also interceding for us. (Rom. 8:33–34)

> Yet now he has reconciled you to himself through the death of Christ in his physical body. As a result, he has brought you into his own presence, and you are holy and blameless as you stand before him without a single fault. (Col. 1:22 NLT)

Because God has placed you in Christ, making you holy and blameless in His sight, Jesus has called you to a brand-new life. A life no longer marred by sin, but baptized by grace—just like the woman caught in the act of adultery.

Thus He says to you . . . and to us . . . *Go and sin no more. I have written a new identity and a new future for you in the dust and dirt of this life.*

2

Diary of a Prostitute Who Loved Much

I have learned something powerful and simple. There is a love that transcends worthlessness and the sinful deeds done in darkness. This is what I shout now. And I am forever changed in light of that love.

Yet love's opposite, lust, wielded its terrible power over me for too many years.

Men had two faces toward me. When others, particularly their wives, were not looking, their eyes held lust. When onlookers surrounded them, they carried disgust. I know both looks well.

Lust and disgust. They had become my companions many years on the streets. If I allowed them to permeate my heart, I would feel like dying nearly every moment. But

I had to continue on. The lust of men had no end, and it paid me well, if you want to know the stark truth.

Would you laugh if I told you my dreams as a little girl? Would you poke fun at my ambitions? What I wanted was so desperately simple—a home, a husband, a passel of children.

One night changed all that.

The air was warm, scented sweet by opening blossoms. Spring intoxicated me at fifteen, enticing me to walk outside in the cool evening so I could think, away from the constant bickering of my siblings. On the ridge above my village, I felt invincible, as if I could command the moon and tell the stars to dance. I sat on a large boulder that night, and let out the breath I had been holding all day long.

Ah sweet Shalom.

Just me and the rising moon in a circle of rare quiet.

I was accustomed to telling God about everything He already knew. I wondered if I bothered the Almighty by prattling on, but then I reasoned if I had children, I would stare rapt at them, the miracle of who they were, and long to hear their dreams and wonderings. So perhaps God sat rapt in the heavens as I declared my frustration, detailed my future, and told Him of the petty frustrations of my day.

"I would like to know what You have for me next," I said to the breeze. "Will my husband have workman hands? Will he be taller than me? Will he love me?" A bird answered back, but nothing more.

And then, a rustle.

From the corner of my vision, I saw a man. He strode toward me in sandaled feet, earthen-colored cloak. He wore a beard and a bemused look. "Seeking a husband, I hear?"

The man's tone hinted at domination, not invitation. I turned inward, searching to find the words to get me out of this situation, but he reached for me, grabbed my arm, and clenched my flesh in his strong hand.

He ripped hair from its roots, until my eyes screamed tears. What I would not give for one of my brothers to find me, to rescue me.

But no such rescue came.

I watched the moon, concentrated on the stars, begged the heavens to come down upon us, but the sky did not fall for me.

The man sneered when he stood up, tall, looming. The moon haloed his head while I wept.

In his hand he held a fistful of hair. "You will not tell a soul," he said. "I kill those who tell."

And I believed him.

I limped back home in the dead of night from the place of my undoing to the place I would exile myself from. I wondered if my parents or brothers or sisters had searched for me. But since they knew my habits of wandering in the evenings, I hoped that, perhaps, they forgot about me, and would be drunk with sleep when I returned.

I tiptoed around their sleeping forms, carefully gathering my things. I refused to bring shame upon this house. There were no secrets in this village. Like hidden sin, they bubble to the surface every time. Someday the dawn of daylight would expose this secret for all its ugly shame. Because of one man's act, I would be rendered a harlot, certainly not a virgin who could be given in marriage.[1]

Every single dream collapsed as I paused to watch my family sleep. I would never have this oasis of calm, never hear the snoring of my husband, the sighing of my first-born, the tossing and turning of my thirdborn.

I traveled far away from my village, then found some-one to shave my head. There, I mourned my patchy skull. But even more than that, I lamented with sackcloth and ashes the life I would never experience. I subsisted on the outskirts of benevolent farmers' fields, gleaning like Ruth, barely eating, scarcely surviving. As my hair grew back, I noticed that look of lust in the eyes of several men in the village. I knew now I was a washed-out rag, good for nothing but to glean and long for food. But I might as well eat. I might as well have some sort of home.

So I exchanged my already-used body for money.

The first time felt like agony, but I kept my tears bottled inside.

The second time, I gritted my teeth.

The third time, I closed my eyes, trying to imagine the moon, the stars—only to remember that night and shud-der inside myself.

The fourth time, I made a choice. I accepted my lot. The reason, perhaps, that God placed me on this earth. I would have to choose a different dream now—to satisfy the hunger of many men, not one. And be paid for my work, handsomely.

From that point onward, I deadened my heart. I pretended I never wanted a family, believed I was meant for something else—a service men needed, I reasoned. I play-acted my way through each encounter, feigning interest, alluring with my eyes though I saw revulsion in theirs.

I never kissed those men, never gave them my soul, my heart.

When a religious leader curried my services, I dared to say the words that merited a firm slap. "We are not unlike each other," I told him. "You pretend to be religiously pious, but instead pay a prostitute to quell your urges. I pretend to be interested in you, but instead I count the money you will give me. You want power through your position. I have power because of mine."

I held sway over many, many men—a strange sort of payback I enjoyed. I could, with one word, cut down a reputation so painstakingly built. Yes, this power I relished.

The dance of prostitution continued many years. I made my money, created a home for myself with fine linens, food for a queen, and perfumes that scented my bedding. I found it to be a fitting joke now, the way the men judged me publicly, yet wanted me privately. I coddled the power of my position and convinced myself I did have the life I always dreamed of.

Except as I grew older by the years, I would no longer be considered pretty. My livelihood hung in a terrible balance, threatened by age and the toll this life took upon my weathered face. My only insurance? The vial of wildly expensive perfume that hung between my breasts.

Some nights, after I completed my work, I would climb the ridge beyond our village, stare at the same moon and stars, and be fifteen years young and blessedly unviolated, full of dreams of family, of joyful life, of a clean heart. I gave these terrible wishes to the wind on those evenings, with an ache that grew deeper than my comfortable life.

I would never, ever be whole. Never clean. Never pure. Never accepted. Certainly never forgiven.

The tears would come slowly in those moments, and I would try not to give in to weeping.

And then I would think, why not start over? Who says I cannot? I would pack up my home and transport myself to another village, only to be dissatisfied with gleaning. Men would find me. They would know whether I possessed powers over them, or perhaps they had heard rumors from other villages, I am not quite sure. But they dazzled me with denarii, and I relieved their urgent needs.

I moved to Nain several Sabbaths ago, in hopes of a new start. Naïvely perhaps. The money I saved from the last village kept me in food and clothing. I survived without giving my body in service, and I refrained from dipping into my perfume, keeping a modest lifestyle. My head began to clear. Perhaps, I thought, I could make my way without selling my body. But the mornings brought hunger. Would I have to sell the perfume for food, for livelihood? It represented all the tears I would not allow myself to cry, enslaved at the hands of hungry men.

I ventured to the central part of Nain in search of figs, coins gripped tightly in my left hand. My stomach rumbled.

In the market the kindly old man known as Elkanah greeted me, eyes dancing. "And how are you today, ma'am?"

Part of me wanted to tell him just how tired I was, how desperately hungry I felt, but instead I answered, "All is well. All is well."

He handed me four figs and winked.

"I can only pay you for three."

"Consider it my tithe," he said. "You need to eat more, and I cannot be the reason your bones jut from your cheeks."

I wanted to hug him, but I kept my distance, telling myself not to tear up at his kindness. I wondered if he knew my secret prostitution and was only being nice to me for this sake.

"You know what I have heard." He touched my arm.

I jerked backwards. He knew?

He lifted his hands heavenward, in surrender. "I am sorry," he said. "I did not mean to startle."

"I am new here," I told Elkanah. "And I do not know who to trust."

He laughed. "I am harmless. And quite withered." He showed me his right hand, curled inward, gnarled by life and crippling disease. "I have heard of a man who heals hands like mine. He seems to love outcasts, those our little society shuns. And he is near!"

He looked through me in that moment, and I turned away.

"His name is Jesus of Nazareth. The exorcisor. The healer. Some say He is the Messiah."

When he said the name Jesus, my heart leapt. But I said nothing.

"I believe He can heal this hand." Elkanah grabbed my attention, looking into my eyes. "And any manner of broken heart."

Impossible, I thought. Too many men. Too many transactions. Too much disease and weariness. I thanked the kind man and made my way toward my home. On the left a crowd formed, dust twirling beneath shuffling feet. In the midst of this crowd stood a man. In sandals. In an earthen cloak. At first I recoiled, remembering the night so many years before. Was He the same? Another man hiding despicable deeds beneath eloquent speech?

I heard a voice from the crowd say, "Tell us more, Jesus."

Jesus. The One who mended broken hearts. I skirted along the side of the crowd as I am used to doing and listened to His words. "To what can I compare the people of this generation? How can I describe them? They are like children playing a game in the public square. They complain to their friends, 'We played wedding songs, and you did not dance, so we played funeral songs, and you did not weep.'"

What did Jesus mean? Perhaps He spoke about expectations unmet, or not reacting as we should in the proper context. Was I like one of those children—playing wedding and funeral songs, hoping for a perfect reaction?

The muffle of voices gave way to the words of Jesus again. "For John the Baptist did not spend his time eating bread or drinking wine, and you say, 'He is possessed by a demon.' The Son of Man, on the other hand, feasts and drinks, and you say, 'He is a glutton and a drunkard, and a friend of tax collectors and other sinners!' But wisdom is shown to be right by the lives of those who follow it."

I had heard of this John who baptized—to some a wild man, to others a saint. To the religious men I have known, he was the former, to the workingmen, the latter. But it was the name of Jesus that stopped me, the thought of Him befriending tax collectors and other sinners. Why would a man of God befriend a tax collector? If this were true, would I qualify as "other sinners"? The reputation of tax collectors far exceeded that of a prostitute. At least we provided a service for money freely given, not stolen. If this Jesus could befriend thieves, would He be my friend too? And could He forgive all I had done?

I followed Jesus several days, gleaning His teachings, always, always on the edge of the crowd, my face veiled. My heart hungered for His words, more than I had lusted after security and the wealth that came from giving myself away. I needed to know that what He said was true. Did He really welcome those who felt unworthy? Or those who had lived in sin for a lifetime—so long they figured they were beyond the reach of forgiveness?

On the Sabbath I watched as my elderly friend Elkanah dared to approach Jesus at the synagogue. I held my breath, kept myself as inconspicuous as I could. But I could not hear what passed between them. So I dared to move closer. The religious teachers argued with Jesus about the Law and what was appropriate to perform on the Sabbath. Elkanah looked nearly angelic as he stood at a slight distance from Jesus, waiting to discover what the Healer would do, while his hand curled inward. Elkanah turned and saw me. He winked.

I shuddered, shrunk away, until I heard the voice of Jesus.

"Come and stand in front of everyone," He told Elkanah. He obeyed.

Jesus looked at the religious leaders, one of whom I had known many times upon my bed. I pulled the veil still tighter over my face.

"I have a question for you," Jesus said. "Does the law permit good deeds on the Sabbath, or is it a day for doing evil? Is this a day to save life or to destroy it?"

I wanted someone to answer, but no one did. Silence reigned.

Jesus gave Elkanah a kindly look that also held exasperation. He looked hard at each of the men accusing Him, then redirected His attention back at Elkanah.

"Hold out your hand," He told my friend.

Elkanah extended his withered hand. It trembled as he did so. Jesus touched the gnarled fist. His eyes held tears, but they smiled too. In an instant, the withered hand opened up like a flower under the springtime sun. Elkanah wept and laughed and danced and flexed his hand, thrusting it skyward.

He thanked Jesus, thanked the Almighty, laughing all the way to me. He pointed to his hand, marveling at the restoration.

"This is how He changes lives," Elkanah said. "From withered to free. I wish that freedom for you."

I let the tears fall at the beauty of my friend's restored hand. And I continued to follow Jesus and His gaggle of disciples for many days, all the while asking God if He could show me somehow if a life such as mine could be restored like that.

As many reclined to hear Him teach on a hillside, I listened too. He turned my way while He spoke and said these words into my soul, a direct answer to my prayer days earlier. He said, "God blesses you who weep now, for in due time you will laugh."

How could that be? I had known far too many nights when I had baptized the hillsides with my tears, but I knew few days of laughter. And yet, every time I heard Jesus speak, I felt that joy might become a possibility for me.

Even me.

He continued speaking, and with each phrase, hope took hold of my heart. I dared to believe there could be a clean start, forgiveness. And as I entertained that wild thought, Jesus said, "Forgive others, and you will be forgiven."

Then my hope died.

I could not forgive that now faceless man who haunted my nightmares and stole my dreams. He did not deserve my forgiveness. He deserved—

With that I looked at my hands, the hands that caressed too many men to count, who had taken their money in exchange for sin. Not only had I transgressed in the sheer act of fornication, but I had encouraged the same sin in other men. The weight of all that dirtiness, all that shame, covered me in that moment. I would never be clean of it.

It was the sort of filth one washes away, only to realize the water used to clean had also been muddy.

Never be set free.

Never understand forgiveness.

Elkanah? He was a kind man with a withered hand who most likely deserved his healing. But me? I deserved every haughty look, every judgmental sentence, every condemnation.

Forgiveness? No.

Still, Jesus spoke of John the Baptist and repentance, of turning away from your sinful lifestyle, of asking for a fresh start. In the quiet of my home that night, I mulled over all the words I heard Jesus say. I contemplated the miracles I witnessed. And as I did, I fell to the floor, utterly weighted down by my sins. They felt like a boulder pinning me to the earth. I counted each sin, then recounted them in detail before God, spilling out all my unworthiness, my failures, my anger.

"Why did that man do that to me?" I asked God, hiccupping between sobs. I heard no answer, but with each declaration, I felt peace that perhaps God had a bigger plan, that He could trump what others had done to me and renew it somehow. I brought my withered, incapable life before God in that down-on-the-ground moment. "Would You restore my life as You renewed the vigor of Elkanah's hand?"

I cannot explain what happened next, except that my soul blossomed.

The shame, vanished.

The fear, gone.

The dirtiness, cleansed.

The anger, dissipated.

I remembered the words of King David about God being my shepherd, preparing a feast in the presence of those who despised me. As I lapped in breaths of freedom air, I felt the cup of my life overflow in gratitude. I finally understood the words of King David when he wrote, "You anoint my head with oil; my cup overflows. Surely goodness and mercy shall follow me all the days of my life, and I shall dwell in the house of the LORD forever." Though I was not royalty or worthy of an anointing, the feeling of it overwhelmed me. I could nearly smell the oil as cleansing poured over my head, over my eyes, my throat, heart.

"God of Heaven's Armies," I prayed, "thank You for welcoming me into Your home like a desired and wanted child."

I stood on shaky legs. As night descended I began to understand Jesus' words about forgiveness because I absolutely experienced it. And in light of that I found that the possibility to forgive others now lived in my heart. I brushed the dust from my face, hands, knees, and began to dance. And cry. And sing. I ran to the outskirts of Nain under a full moon and twirled under its shadow a free woman, so blessedly alive it nearly scared me to death.

But one thing I did know: Jesus ushered in this surprising change, and I would spend all my strength thanking Him. I touched the flask of precious perfume I held for safekeeping, knowing what I must do. I would bless Jesus with everything I had because He had become everything to me. He had given me life—and He deserved my sacrifice. What was two years' wages, what was any amount of money, next to a heart made clean?

The next day I discovered Jesus in a crowd. I wanted to rush at Him then with my gift, but propriety and a hint of fear held me back.

To my right I heard one man, a Pharisee, clear his throat. The others turned to see him standing to the side, proud, tall, preening. "Come to my home and eat," he said to Jesus. It sounded more like command than invitation, and I sensed a hint of anger in his voice, muffled only by smiling lips. At a distance I followed the crowd, orienting myself to the twists and turns of this part of the village, counting steps down crooked dusty paths until I noticed the home where Jesus entered.

I knew better than to ask for entrance, for it would be denied to a woman of ill repute. I had long heard the whisperings around the other places I lived to know there is no small village, not even Nain, where my deeds and reputation could not follow. But I did not care. Because once I saw Jesus reclining at the table, I became overwhelmed at His beauty and the revolution He had begun in my heart.

I snuck into the crowded home, preferring to inch along the periphery, still afraid.

That is, until He spoke.

His voice resurrected my willpower, and I found Him, collapsing at His feet. I intended to anoint His feet with my perfume, but I found myself overtaken with emotion and I wept. His feet, now unsandaled, were dirt-encrusted from the day's walk, and no one had cleaned them. My tears ran over the dust, eddying into tiny pools beneath His toes. If tears could clean such dirty feet, there was hope for an unclean woman like me. This I knew.

Though earth-stained, I marveled at the beauty of His feet. They had taken Him to people who had lost everything—their health, their hands, their livelihoods, their reputation. These feet brought Him to Nain, to me. I could not help but do the thing no prostitute dares to do.

I kissed.

His feet.

I heard gasps, but I did not care.

These beautiful feet deserved lavish affection. I wondered why no one else sat at the Master's feet, blessing Him with the same kiss. Was no one else moved by the wonder of Jesus?

I had left my expensive silks and linens at home, so I had nothing to cleanse His feet. But I did have my hair. I unbound my tresses to more guffaws, no doubt the wagging of heads at this indignity I committed. Unbinding hair made me naked in these men's eyes—no doubt a horrific scandal. I should have worried about committing such an audacious act amidst the holy, but all I could think about was Jesus' need for dried, clean feet, and my insatiable need to thank Him for loving me.

So I continued, unhindered, grabbing fistfuls to smear away the caked-on mud.

Jesus demanded nothing from me. He reclined, blessedly silent. He simply welcomed my adoration without expecting something in return, so unlike nearly every man I had known.

The tension in the room thickened. I took the perfume, and poured my security upon His feet. The room permeated the scent's brilliance and beauty. My worship, that perfume. My worthiness. My livelihood. The liquid that guaranteed my wealth. I kissed His now perfume-anointed feet.

I worked with such fervor that I chose to forget about the stares of others. Until I looked up and the proud Pharisee glared at me, shock and anger in his icy stare. I had humiliated him in front of Jesus. In his home, no less.

I stiffened. Looked at my hands, nearly forgetting all that Jesus had done for me and in me. I felt five years old and foolish. But Jesus touched my hand as if to say, "Wait, child."

Jesus looked at Simon. "I have something to say to you," He said.

"Go ahead, Teacher." Simon glared at me again.

"A man loaned money to two people—500 pieces of silver to one and 50 pieces to the other. But neither of them could repay him, so he kindly forgave them both, canceling their debts. Who do you suppose loved him more after that?"

That beautiful, terrible, empowering word: forgave. I felt it pound my heart, resurrecting my hope. Mine had been a 500-piece-of-silver life, to be sure.

But Simon shifted. "I suppose the one for whom he canceled the larger debt." His words sounded as if he did not want to say them. And he said them while looking through me.

"That is right," Jesus said. He turned, looked at me without lust, without disgust. "Look at this woman kneeling here. When I entered your home, you did not offer Me water to wash the dust from My feet, but she has washed them with her tears and wiped them with her hair. You did not greet Me with a kiss, but from the time I first came in, she has not stopped kissing My feet. You neglected the courtesy of olive oil to anoint My head, but she has anointed My feet with rare perfume."

In the company of Jesus' words, I came undone—again. Because He allowed me an extreme privilege. He had anointed me with His healing when I knelt in the dust, and now I had anointed Him. Would His cup overflow too? This Jesus who healed and loved and welcomed, He dignified my scented offering. How could this be so?

Jesus touched a strand of my hair. I did not recoil. I remembered what the evil man ripped from my head, the raw patch of skin that screamed pain. So much shame that man forced onto me. And so much sin I committed in the aftermath. And yet grace made Jesus talk to me, accepting my small offering. I had been unclean. Unloved. Unwanted. Unworthy.

But no longer.

Jesus quieted the table. "I tell you, her sins—and they are many—have been forgiven, so she has shown me much love. But a person who is forgiven little shows only little love."

Jesus looked at me, intently, and smiled. He released what I had formerly squelched. Potential. Freedom. Cleanness. Hope.

THE DAY I MET JESUS

"Your sins are forgiven," He reminded me. A clear declaration of the supernatural change that had happened as I groveled in the dust last night and spilled my story clear out.

I stood.

The tears continued down my face. I dropped the perfume flask, shattering it on the hardened earth. I felt the weight of the stares of the men in the room, but I did not allow their disgust to inform my worth. Jesus forgave me. Blessedly, shockingly so. He welcomed me into His house, a child well loved.

A furor erupted around the table. The men questioned among themselves, "Who is this man, that He goes around forgiving sins?"

Who indeed? He was God with human feet. Because of Him, I became a woman forgiven much, and I would choose to love much. Not many men, but One. Passionately for the rest of my life.

"Your faith has saved you," Jesus said as I neared the door. "Go in shalom."

And I did.

My tears are dry now, and I sit under the moonlit night with joy reverberating through me. As stars light the sky, I remember another thing Jesus said to the crowds right after He spoke of forgiveness. "Give and you will receive," He said. "Your gift will return to you in full—pressed down, shaken together to make room for more, running over, and poured into your lap. The amount you give will determine the amount you get back."

THE SACRED TEXT

When one of the Pharisees invited Jesus to have dinner with him, he went to the Pharisee's house and reclined at the table. A woman in that town who lived a sinful life learned that Jesus was eating at the Pharisee's house, so she came there with an alabaster jar of perfume. As she stood behind him at his feet weeping, she began to wet his feet with her tears. Then she wiped them with her hair, kissed them and poured perfume on them.

When the Pharisee who had invited him saw this, he said to himself, "If this man were a prophet, he would know who is touching him and what kind of woman she is—that she is a sinner."

Jesus answered him, "Simon, I have something to tell you."

"Tell me, teacher," he said.

"Two people owed money to a certain moneylender. One owed him five hundred denarii, and the other fifty. Neither of them had the money to pay him back, so he forgave the debts of both. Now which of them will love him more?"

Simon replied, "I suppose the one who had the bigger debt forgiven."

"You have judged correctly," Jesus said.

Then he turned toward the woman and said to Simon, "Do you see this woman? I came into your house. You did not give me any water for my feet, but she wet my feet with her tears and wiped them with her hair. You did not give me a kiss, but this woman, from the time I entered, has not stopped kissing my feet. You did not put oil on my head, but she has poured perfume on my feet. Therefore, I tell you, her many sins have been forgiven—as her great love has shown. But whoever has been forgiven little loves little."

Then Jesus said to her, "Your sins are forgiven."

The other guests began to say among themselves, "Who is this who even forgives sins?"

Jesus said to the woman, "Your faith has saved you; go in peace."

—Luke 7:36–50

WALKING IT OUT

The story of the sinful woman who anointed Jesus in the house of a Pharisee shows us yet another aspect of the true Lover of our souls.

In order to better understand the force of the narrative, imagine two children.

One is a young boy raised in a strong religious home. His name is Simon. He's a diligent young lad, devoted to God and the Torah (Law of Moses).

Simon joins the party of the Pharisees, the most influential sect in Judaism—separatists who carefully follow the food and purity laws of the Torah. They are deeply devoted to knowing, interpreting, and applying the Law of Moses to the life of Israel. They are zealous about purifying the nation.

Given their preoccupation with purity, the Pharisees will have nothing to do with sinful people. They view themselves as the experts at sin management. They become the self-appointed, self-anointed, self-righteous monitors of God's kingdom who distance themselves from anyone who practices sin.

In their view, they belong to a special class of people: Non-sinners. So they think, anyway.

The other child is a little girl. Precious, innocent, and beautiful. But things go horribly wrong in her upbringing, and she ends up giving her body in exchange for money. She becomes a woman of the night, a prostitute, a harlot.[2] Good Jews despise her. She's defiled and unclean. The dregs of society.

Neither child realizes it, but they will soon collide. One day they will meet as adults in the most surprising of circumstances. And as a result, one of their lives will change forever.

That's the backdrop to this remarkable story.

A Collision of Two Classes

Scholars point out that Simon was relatively wealthy because he could host a large banquet in his home.

Strikingly, the young prophet who reclined in Simon's home that day was the very God whom Simon and his friends had been trying to serve all their lives.

Stop and consider that for a moment.

The woman who entered Simon's home was the little girl who was once a precious, innocent, beautiful child. She was all grown up now—yet not so gracefully.

No one had invited her in, yet she unabashedly entered the home of Simon the Pharisee, only to fall under the judgmental eye of his friends.

In the first-century world, people's homes weren't private as they now are in the modern West. A person could walk straight into someone's house unopposed, even if they were never invited. So it wasn't unusual for this woman to enter into Simon's home. The unusual aspect is her stature in society.

Look at the contrast. The woman is a dirty prostitute—a common whore by social status, ritually impure and utterly contagious in her impurity.[3] The home she's entered belongs to a so-called pure and clean Pharisee. She entered as an intruder—and a defiling one at that.

Pure Righteousness Meets Self-Righteousness

We can presume that this woman had already heard Jesus teach. She discovered Jesus' whereabouts with the intent to anoint Him as an act of gratitude. But when she entered Simon's home and saw the prophet up close and personal, she became overwhelmed.

In the first-century, people reclined on low couches at banquets, leaning on the left arm with their head toward the table and their body stretched away from it. So the woman didn't sit near the table.

The unbinding of her hair must have horrified Simon and outraged his Pharisee friends. In the first-century Jewish world, the act of a woman unbinding her hair in public bordered on scandalous. It would be similar to a woman going topless in public today. Men would deem it to be erotic.

To attend to someone's feet was a menial task, one that was usually assigned to a slave. Some scholars point out that she would have appeared to be fondling Jesus' feet like a prostitute or a slave girl providing sexual favors. Either way, the Pharisees would have considered her actions at the table to be shamelessly erotic, socially awkward, and profoundly inappropriate.

In that day, women wore tiny vials about the length of a finger, made of limestone (or occasionally glass), containing perfume (pistic nard), that they carried on a leather thong around their necks. However, from the Greek word that Luke uses in this narrative, the perfume was probably contained in a long flask that the woman purchased with her prostitution income. It represented her livelihood, likely earned through giving nearly everything of herself to satisfy her clients' sexual demands.

To Simon's mind, the godly do not associate with the wicked. Hence why he thought to himself, *If this man were a prophet, He would know that she's a sinner, and He wouldn't allow this shameful behavior and disgraceful act.*

It's significant that Jesus didn't stop her overt affection. And He never reproved her for it.

The Lord knew exactly who she was. And He also knew exactly who Simon was. In fact, He perceived the very thoughts of the Pharisee.

Pause and notice.

In the eyes of the only perfect Man who ever lived, this sinful woman *loved* God. And a self-righteous Pharisee *judged* God . . . as well as the person who lavishly loved Him. Without realizing it, Simon and his friends criticized the very God they thought they were serving.

A Prophet Indeed

As always, Jesus kept His poise in the midst of awkward situations. On the one hand, He allowed a sinful woman to perform an outrageous act of affection in a very

71

public manner. On the other, He observed a self-righteous Pharisee engaging in an outrageous act of judgment upon Him.

What Jesus said to Simon denuded the Pharisee's self-righteous delusion. After Jesus exposed Simon's serious breach of the laws of hospitality, Jesus dropped the bomb: "Simon, this sinful woman loves Me very much because she's been forgiven very much. But you love Me very little because you believe you are beyond needing forgiveness."

Because Jesus is a prophet—One who represents God—the implication was that Simon not only loved God little, but he barely knew Him!

And while Simon didn't approve of this woman, God didn't approve of Simon.

You see, God doesn't approve of those who see themselves as part of the class of "non-sinners."

> If we claim to be without sin, we deceive ourselves and the truth is not in us. (1 John 1:8)

> Here is a trustworthy saying that deserves full acceptance: Christ Jesus came into the world to save sinners—of whom I am the worst. (1 Tim. 1:15)

> But the tax collector stood at a distance. He would not even look up to heaven, but beat his breast and said, "God, have mercy on me, a sinner." (Luke 18:13)

The lens of self-righteousness saw the woman's behavior as erotic, shameful, and sinful. The lens of true righteousness saw it as beautiful, sacred, and gracious.

These two lenses still exist today . . . even among Christians.

The Upside-Down Kingdom

All throughout the Gospels, Jesus Christ is shown to be the friend (and defender) of sinners (Luke 7:34). In this story, we find Him to be eating, drinking, and befriending a female sinner.

Jesus welcomed the tax collectors, the thieves, the prostitutes, and the adulterers into His kingdom. For this reason, the Lord consistently violated social taboos to reach out to those who the culture marginalized (Luke 7:1–10) economically (Luke 7:11–17), religiously (Luke 7:24–34), and morally (Luke 7:36–50).

But He leveled his severest critique to the religious, self-righteous, morally upright. (See the Lord's bone-chilling rebukes to such people in Matthew 23.)

These self-righteous folks disqualified themselves from the kingdom of God—the kingdom they thought they were building through their outwardly pristine behavior.

This truth is part of the astonishing reversal of the kingdom of God. And it goes against every expectation that the people of Israel had about what the world would look like when God's kingdom materialized on earth.

No one expected that the kingdom would look like prostitutes forgiven, tax collectors received, adulterers rescued, divorcees honored, traitors absolved—each of them receiving a new life and a high place in God's house, all because

73

of the amazing grace, unfailing mercy, and abundant redemption of Israel's true Messiah.

Now let's put a self-righteous Christian in that room with this woman, Simon, and God enfleshed. What might that person ask or say?

"Lord, did she ask for forgiveness?"

"I'm not sure she repented. I want to interrogate her to make sure she did."

"I did not hear her say she was sorry for committing such awful, heinous sins."

"I can never understand how someone could give their body for money. That is one of the worst sins a person can commit!"

Such words and thoughts can only come forth from those who have been captured by the spirit of a Pharisee.

And we have not so learned Jesus Christ.[4]

The sober reality is that self-righteousness will bar many from the kingdom of God.

Behold this woman, sinful like the rest of us, but perhaps in a different way. She chose to love Jesus at great cost to herself. She poured out her devotion and her economic livelihood upon Him unashamedly and outrageously in the presence of self-righteous Pharisees.

Luke closes the curtains on this scene with Jesus commending the woman, announcing that she has indeed been forgiven and that her faith has saved her. He then tells her to go in peace. What hope-filled, beautiful words for a woman who did not understand shalom in her daily life.

Jesus did not imply that her actions earned forgiveness. They resulted from her forgiveness, and He pronounced aloud for all to hear what was already true. Her love became proof that she had already been forgiven. Her act of affection was her response to God's unfailing grace.

Point: True faith is demonstrated when we allow ourselves to receive God's generous forgiveness in Christ. And the proof of that faith is love. What is more, faith brings forth peace.

Notice that Jesus didn't invite this woman to be part of His apostolic band. No, she had to return to her life of conflict and tension. Not as a prostitute, but as someone who used to be. And she had to find another way to earn income.

But Jesus said to her, "Go in peace," which literally means "go *into* peace." Yes, her life wouldn't be easy right away or maybe not at all. But she encountered the Prince of Peace, and He sent her on her way "into peace." Indeed, salvation leads a person on the path of peace (Luke 1:79). So love reveals faith, and faith brings forth peace.

The gospel of the New Testament is highlighted in this scene. It doesn't matter how great your sins are; God's grace is big enough to forgive and cleanse them.

Later in his Gospel, Luke gives us two stories that Jesus told which underscore the insidious problem of self-righteousness: The prodigal son (Luke 15) and the Pharisee and tax collector (Luke 18).

Christian therapist and professor Dr. Dan Allender once said, "Self-righteousness is more decadent than the worst sexual sin."[5] The story in Luke 7 underscores that point.

Jesus and the Pharisees

To better understand Simon and his friends, let's take a closer look at Jesus and His encounters with the Pharisees. One reason why Christ had so much conflict with the Pharisaical party is because they were committed to God's revelation in the Torah, but their interpretation of it had shifted radically.

This became a problem because the Pharisees disdained any other interpretation of the Torah except their own. They also gave in to a strong strain of jealousy, making Jesus a target of their anger.

Here are some examples of the conflict that Jesus had with the Pharisees:

- The Pharisees opposed John the Baptist and Jesus for their kingdom message (Matt. 3:7).
- The Pharisees opposed Jesus and His followers for their Sabbath observances (Matt. 12:2).
- The Pharisees wanted Jesus to give them a sign (Matt. 12:38).
- The Pharisees opposed Jesus and His followers over hand-washing rituals (Matt. 15:1–20).
- The Pharisees taught things that Jesus criticized as opposing God's will (Matt. 16:6, 12).
- The Pharisees had a righteousness that Jesus said was inadequate (Matt. 5:20).
- The Pharisees opposed Jesus and His followers for eating with the wrong people (Matt. 9:11).
- The Pharisees had a different practice of fasting (Matt. 9:14).

- The Pharisees accused Jesus of casting out demons in league with Satan (Matt. 9:34).
- The Pharisees tested Jesus often (Matt. 16:1; 19:3; John 8:6).
- The Pharisees wanted Jesus "put away" and Jesus was aware of it (Matt. 22:15; 21:33–45).
- The Pharisees were denounced by Jesus for being hypocrites (Matt. 23).[6]

Five Important Lessons

All told, there are five big lessons we can glean from this story.

1. You will never know if self-righteousness lurks in your heart until you see someone you regard as "sinful" audaciously loving Jesus. How you react to that situation will uncover what's deep within your heart.

2. Self-righteousness will disqualify you from the kingdom of God. Serving God, as Simon performed his entire life, doesn't score brownie points with the Almighty. Humility and treating others the way you want to be treated in all circumstances is what Jesus is after. This, in fact, fulfills the entire law and the prophets (Matt. 7:12).

3. It doesn't matter what you've done or how bad you've failed, Jesus Christ is bigger than all your foul-ups, and His mercy and grace loom larger than any sin you've ever committed.

4. Ultimately, your God is after love. Beyond everything else, even service, He wishes to be loved (Matt. 22:37–38). You are His beloved.

5. In the upside-down kingdom of Jesus, if you deem yourself to be part of the class called "non-sinners" and judge those who are not like you, then you're dangerously out of favor with God.

We all should be impressed by the sinful woman. She embodies the depths of fallen humanity. Yet Jesus loved her and forgave her. And despite her unbecoming life, she knew that Jesus was a friend of sinners . . . which means that He was *her* friend.

So the next time you feel condemnation over your past sins, mistakes, and failures, remember this: A sinful woman extravagantly loved the Lord of glory—*your Lord*—in the house of a Pharisee.

And He was not ashamed of her.

Neither is He ashamed of you.

You are His beloved child. So take your rightful place and rest joyfully there.

> Both the one who makes people holy and those who are made holy are of the same family. So Jesus is not ashamed to call them brothers and sisters. (Heb. 2:11)

3

Diary of a Desperate Samaritan Woman

I have never wanted to write my story because no happy ending existed. Besides, who would want to read my woeful words, and why? Instead my life played like Job's tragedy without his restoration, tied with a twisted thread of betrayal.[1]

Always, always, I would think on the years past, saddened by the tangle of them, thinking God had forgotten my life, my dreams. My stomach kept itself in knots while people pointed and wagged their heads.

But now.

Oh, glorious, grace-awakening now!

I write these words with wild expectation, with sudden joy, because a man told my story to me straight, and, with that, changed its ending forever.

But before I write of my parched soul now quenched, I must take you back to the moment I withered.

There had been an old era, when water meant life to me. My first husband Hezron had met me by Jacob's well in those carefree halcyon days, the well that I ventured to today. He playfully called it his well, though we both knew the real origin. His words still sang through me: "You are more spectacular than the sunrise."

I blushed under such words and said nothing in response. Could he really find me so attractive? His eyes affirmed so. I believed, like a naïve girl, that he spoke truth. I blossomed in the light of it.

"And our children," he said with the same affection, "will carry your beauty and my wit." With that, he winked.

I dared to whisper, "I hope so," but the dry wind carried my words.

Like those around us, parents arranged our marriage. But I had no parents, no *ketubah* to give his family. "Beautiful but moneyless," he told me. But when he said it, his eyes sparkled and his smile dimpled. "You are my *ketubah*, my sweet dowry promise," he said then, holding my face in his hands.

I drank in Hezron's words like the thirstiest girl in Samaria. With a mother and father sleeping long in their graves on the hillside, I lived under the shadow of an angry aunt. Hezron's love gave me hope and a means to escape her servitude. We secreted away to marry, despite the protests of others. Once we settled into our home, people began to accept us.

Hezron's love lasted four months. Writing it now still brings heartache.

When my belly did not swell with child, his face soured and his brow furrowed.

After six months, his voice harshened. "What kind of womb refuses my gift?" His questions were not meant as an invitation to conversation. They became angry declarations of my unworthiness. With as much love as he first had, sacrificing his reputation to be with me, he now hated me with the same vigor. He could not even look my way. He would not. But he would have me nonetheless.

Nine months passed since we married, and Hezron snapped like a dry twig underfoot. He lifted his hand, threatened to hit me, only to recoil, then cry, then beg me to forgive him for such threats. He bounced between madman and saint. I learned to read each mood, either cowering or welcoming him. Always seducing him to bed in hopes of winning his affection through the gift of a baby.

The family he betrayed by whisking me away for marriage became another Caesar in his life. They mercilessly tore at me with their words, throwing around "worthless" and "barren" like a farmer tosses seeds. Those words implanted themselves into my heart and grew into acacia trees, monuments of my worthlessness.

I became desperate to bear Hezron's child. I visited midwives with special potions. I stood behind mandrake plants. But like Rachel, my hopes died. I prayed to the God of my ancestors, bargaining with Him to please have mercy upon my womb. But He fell as silent as my husband had become.

For a full year we endured my empty womb. On our anniversary, Hezron touched my stomach, his hand weighted on my abdomen. He shook his head. "You, an unfit wife." Four chilling words given as if he were evaluating livestock—cold, hard, detached.

"I am praying," I said.

"The Almighty has closed your womb for a reason. To give me permission to be free of you." He spat his condemnation, and I received it as daggers into my already obliterated heart. I had failed him. God had failed me.

Then Hezron thrust a parchment my way—a "Certificate of Divorce," already signed. The law of the land. A decree proving my barrenness. "I am doing you a favor," he said. "You can live free."

Except that *free* meant homelessness, emptiness—an undying thirst for the love he once had for me, now dried up in the draught of Hezron's wind-shifted affections.

On the morning of the divorce, I stood under an angry sun, beneath the fickle affections of a God who denied my prayers. Barefooted, I walked alone to our trysting place, that terrible well that began with hope, but ended on the heels of bereavement.

Hezron had no legal reason to give me any money when he dismissed me. Since I had no *ketubah*, I used what would have been my dowry on burial sites years ago when my parents succumbed to the fever. And now I stood at the well, barren and without resource.

As the years marched by, I picked up small jobs, gathering sticks, cooking for women whose bellies produced babies aplenty. I lived as a ghost with dreams, watching others live my hope of family, but never participating. "Worthless" and "barren" embodied who I became. I lived my life with head down, empty eyes never meeting a soul.

The small jobs dried up, and I forced myself to move to a nearby village. I naively hoped that a fresh start would mean a new life. So I married again, hoping to quell the pain deep inside of me. I walked this earth to simply be beholden to a man—however he saw fit. When my womb remained empty, my second husband grabbed me by the hair and threw me into the streets.

No one wants a barren woman, no matter how much she gives. This lesson pierced my soul like a flint knife. Two more husbands became temporary. They cycled into my life, then out again as each one discovered my secret. I longed to distance myself from the memory of Hezron, the well, the one small moment I felt love.

Judah changed everything. He found me weeping, bereft of joy, as I picked up firewood on the outskirts of civilization. My hands dusty, my eyes wet, I only saw two sandaled feet as I knelt on the earth, pulling a large branch from scrub.

"Why is a lovely woman like you crawling so close to the ground? Solomon's palace would not suffice such a face." He shielded his eyes from the sun, then coughed.

I looked at him, tall as timber. Shook my head. "I am making my way. Gathering wood is what I do."

"I am Judah." He extended his hand to me and pulled me to my feet. Such easy effort.

I wiped my hands on my tunic. "And I am dusty."

We walked back to the village that evening as the sun faded to pink and blue, then deep purple. I told him my story, and he told me his. Life had broken him—his wife taking her last breath as she pushed a stillborn into this cruel world.

Later, as he asked to marry me, I put my hand up as if to halt him. "I am barren. I can give you no children. I have told this to you already."

"I want a wife," Judah said, "not a mother."

We married quietly and commenced our companioned life together, measured in happy days, conversation, and hushed dreams.

Except that God severed Judah's dreams on this earth. The cough I had noticed in our brief courtship monstered into blood-soaked cloths lifted to dry lips. I loved him all those one hundred and eighteen days, loved him like my own life. And when he bled his last breath, all my vitality drained from me. I haunted the hills—unawake and dead of heart.

I considered exiling myself to Palestine, in the land of the Jews. I had heard rumors of a man who welcomed outcasts, who was kind to widows, who fed thousands. Perhaps He would dignify me. But my brief foray to that land only ended in slanderous rants and racial epithets. Such hatred compelled me back to my people.

In all, five Samaritan husbands had me. Four husbands used my body, then dismissed me. Only one loved me, but my happiness died with him. I shook my fist at the Almighty, daring Him to take my life and be over with it. Why should I remain here on this earth? Without a child, I had no legacy, no hope, no reason to live. There existed none to carry on my traits or my lineage or my sorry story.

What beckoned me back to Sychar where I write my tale? One enticing man and the graves of my parents. When this new man told me where he lived, I remembered the comfort I used to feel visiting my parents on the hillside. He used all of Hezron's words—words like *beautiful*, *love*, and *want*. He seduced me, only to recoil against me in the aftermath. "You are so very safe," he said.

"What do you mean?" I said as I rose up from his sleeping mat, propping my chin on my shaking hand. The shame inside of me burned. Never before had I slept with a man who was not my husband. Half of me worried God would strike me dead; the other half did not care if He did. My life mirrored my womb.

"I am married," he said.

I did not think my heart could break any more, but with those words it shattered into dread.

"But you are useful to me. You are alone, no?"

"Yes, I am alone." Four more words—a declaration of my life.

"And you need food?" He traced his rough hand over the diminishing curve of my hip where the bone protruded.

"Yes." But what I wanted to say was, "I need more than food. More than water. More than shelter."

"You will be my worker," he said. "Live within my house. Take care of my children. Do the work so my wife will not have to labor. And then in the evening . . ."

I knew what he meant. I did not argue with myself whether this would be good or bad. It was simply my lot. To be used. To live for the sake of another, losing myself, my dreams, and my desires completely. A barren widowed woman could hope for no more.

This morning, I tried to shake the dark memories from my head. They played like cautionary tales during nightmares, only to retell themselves in the light of day. With those memories in mind, I grabbed the empty vessel and made the hot, dusty trek to Hezron's terrible well—the place where betrayal entered my life.

I walked with the shame of my past and the guilt of my present—like a heavy camel's skin pressed on sweaty shoulders during the heat of day. I could not remove the weight. I could not escape it.

My body memorized the routine: Walk the dusty road, head down, drop the earthen vessel into the well's deep throat, and lug and lurch its contents home—only to perform the same duty again and again and again. All under the watchful stare of the unrelenting sun.

I trudged there, alone at the noon hour, as was my custom. I dared not draw water in the morning like the other women—to avoid their snickers and stares. They gossiped my current story to death. Every nuance. Even the little children knew; they held up five fingers as reminder of my husbands. Old women shook their heads at me when I walked the town.

Men leered.

I have heard it said that a barren woman must always send herself to get water because she has no children to bear the weight of labor. Halfway to the well, I wondered again (was it the hundredth time?), why am I here in Samaria? What is the reason God placed me on this sullen earth? Does He create people simply to be used and abused? Has His favor shone only on the Jews? Only on the strong? Only on men? Only on women whose wombs produced babies? He certainly did not shine upon me, even as the sun relentlessly accosted me on my long, lonely walk.

I did not know then what I shout with joy now: God loves the weak.

When I arrived, the usually vacant well had a visitor. A man, sitting near the well's mouth. No horse or camel accompanied Him, so I wondered if He had traveled on foot by Himself.

I sighed. His silhouette brought me back to Hezron's dancing eyes and the flutter of my heart in this very spot. Days long stolen. With the sun-washed hillside around Him and the noonday sun shining on the top of His head, He sat perfectly still, completely at peace, it seemed. He did not stand when I entered the circle of the well. Instead, He seemed like a fixture there, a statue that had always been erected.

I rubbed my eyes.

He lingered there, still quiet under a treeless sky, His clothes rumpled from days upon days of travel, it seemed.

As I neared the man, His garments revealed that He was a Jew. But Jews did not journey alone through Samaria. He sat quietly there like He waited for someone.

He looked up, finally, His eyes tired. And yet—more alive than any man's eyes I had seen. I thought to myself, can eyes dance? Can they smile? Sing? Because this man's eyes performed all three while welcoming me to this desolate spot of earth. I said nothing to Him, but He held my gaze. A bead of sweat meandered down His face, but He did not wipe it away. The day mustered to swelter us both.

I dropped my dipper into the deep well.

As I drew near, He turned toward me and looked deeply into my eyes. I had a strange feeling that He knew me. He smiled confidently, paused, cleared His throat, and reached out His hand. "Would you please give Me a drink?" His voice sounded parched, nearly dried up. But it was His words that stunned me to silence.

What kind of holy man dared to talk to me in public? But not just any man—a Jew, as His accent gave his lineage away. A Jewish man talking to me? Wanting only water and nothing more?

Jews had treated my people like dogs, as utter outcasts to their exclusivity on the Almighty. And here this tired man stooped to ask me for a drink. I looked around, wondering if this were a trap.

I heard rumors of Jewish holy men entrapping women like me in compromising situations.

I swallowed hard, my tongue thick in my mouth, but I could not hold back my curiosity. "You are a Jew, and I am a Samaritan. How can you ask me for a drink?" What I really thought: *You Jews will not even talk to Samaritans. Unless, perhaps you want something from us.*

But something about this man prevented those words from leaving my mouth. I saw kindness in His eyes. And I heard compassion in the timbre of His voice, something so compelling and alien that I could not let my sarcasm out.

"If you knew God's gift and who I am," He said, "you would be asking Me for living water and I would give it to you."

A rather arrogant thing to say, seeing that He had brought nothing to draw water. "Sir," I said, "this well is over one hundred feet deep, and You have no wooden dipper and no flaxen cord. Where are You going to get this living water?"

I wanted Him to know I considered the patriarch Jacob my father just as the Jews claim him to be. I have always wanted to tell a Jew that we Samaritans are not half-breeds like they say we are, so I asked, "Are You greater than our father Jacob who dug this well and drank from it?" As I said those words, I remembered the face of Hezron. For the first time in twelve years, I recalled the kindness he once had. Coupled with the kindness of this man, I wondered if perhaps He would love me.

He gestured toward the well. "If you keep coming to this well, you will always thirst, but if you drink the water I offer you, you will never thirst again. In fact, the water that I give will flow from within you forever."

I did not understand what He said—how can water flow from within a person? Water came from the earth, simple as that. But He spoke so confidently, with a spark of love radiating from His eyes, and I felt a sense of care and acceptance coming from Him that I had experienced only from dear, dear Judah.

But life had hardened my heart like clay earth, wholly parched, drained of all its life blood, baked impenetrable by hatred and rejection. I wanted this man's magic water for some temporary relief. I sighed, then looked upon His face. "Sir, give me this water so that I will not get thirsty and have to keep coming here to draw water." Oh how I meant those words. And for a sacred second, I believed this man would give me exactly what I wanted.

"Go, call your husband and come back." The wind inside me, the pneuma, exhaled into the hot, thick air. So there was a special trick to receive such a blessing? I had to have a husband. Little in my life made sense. He sliced open the biggest wound in my heart with His words. I dropped my head and whispered, "I have no husband."

Silence.

I waited for His judgment and withdrawal. He would abandon me as all the others had. Or sneer. Or expose me.

But strangely, He did not move. So utterly peaceful like a calmed sea.

He simply drew my attention in a way that wooed me. He smiled and said, "You are right when you say you have no husband. The fact is, you have had five husbands, and the man you now have is not your husband. So what you have just said is quite true."

I froze.

How could He possibly know that? And why would He so brazenly say these things out loud? The shame inside me warmed my face, blushing my expression. I said nothing, trying to understand how this man knew my story.

I realized that the Jews may be right and prophets exist. Was He a holy prophet, yet one with heart? After all, He offered me living water all the while knowing my story. Would He recoil and shift to angry judgment, grab my hair at the scalp and throw me to the ground? Would He use me for His pleasure and gain?

Kindness played no role in my life. Anyone acting kind only wanted something from me. Instead of wallowing in that inevitability with this man, I changed the topic of conversation. "We Samaritans worship on Mount Gerizim and you Jews worship on Mount Zion. Which one of us is correct?"

"Miss," He said, "believe me, a time is coming when you will worship the Father neither on this mountain nor in Jerusalem.[2] You Samaritans worship what you do not know; we worship what we do know, for salvation is from the Jews."

The rebuke was kind, but He spoke with authority. Nevertheless, I thought, *Always the Jews. Always their special place in God's heart. Never Samaritans.* Perhaps this is why my story is sad? I belonged to an unfavored race? These thoughts stirred me, but I did not voice them.

I sat down near the well to hear the rest of His words. He continued, holding my eyes with His. "Yet a time is coming and has now come when the true worshipers will worship the Father in the Spirit and in truth, for they are the kind of worshipers the Father seeks."

When He said *seeks*, my insides harkened, pregnant with love. Could it be—could it really be that God seeks me to be His worshiper? A five-time-married Samaritan now sleeping with another woman's husband? Why would He notice me? But the man's demeanor toward me seemed to indicate the irresistible truth: I am sought.

"God is spirit." He pointed skyward and smiled. "And His worshipers must worship in the Spirit and in truth."

We Samaritans do not believe in prophets after Moses. Except for the one prophet who we were all waiting for. A prophet like Moses himself. The Jews call Him *the Messiah*. We call Him *Taheb*, the Restorer. "When the Messiah comes," I told Him, "He will explain all of these deep things to us."

"I am the Messiah."

Could it be? The stirring inside me believed it, but to be honest, fear prevented me from rejoicing in this revelation. Those four words strung together would change my story forever. The Restorer of the world revealed His identity to me.

At that moment, voices sounded nearby. The man's companions arrived—His disciples, I surmised. They shot judgment my way, and I could feel the words they did not voice. *Why were you talking to a Samaritan? And a woman no less?*

Still drunk from His *Taheb* declaration, I made a choice to shrug off their quiet accusations. In that moment, He satiated my lifelong thirst—as if clear cool water drenched me refreshed in the heat of day. It baptized my head, rushed down my throat, settled in my stomach, and permeated my thirsty heart.

Anchored to the dusty earth, I knew this longed-for truth: I am loved. So very, utterly noticed. Picked. Wanted. Despite my story. Or maybe because of it? I am not sure. But one thing I am assured of is this: God saw fit to notice me, to make Himself known to me quietly at the place of my betrayal and shame. Living Water met me at high noon.

I heard the Messiah laugh as He watched this transformation unfold in me. While evil had taken a lifetime to destroy me, this man took mere moments to re-story me.

His eyes laughed (and danced and sang). We shared a knowing look, as if He saw the tragedy of my story in its entirety and resurrected it to new purpose—and then He said, "Dare to live your life well." What tragedy happened in the doldrums of my past has now become a wellspring of grace, covering all the shame, sin, and a lifetime of accumulated regret. Under the hot sun, I drank in this grace of a new life, gulped it deep, clasping my hands to my chest because I felt my heart would overflow its borders and spill out onto the crowd.

One man motioned to the Messiah, then called Him Jesus.

Jesus. Such a common name for a man bent on blessing us all.

And in that moment, I knew this sweet gift of living water was not merely meant for me, but for all of Sychar. I found my feet, and with eyes wide open, I ran home to Sychar, my heart full of living, breathing, enlivening water. Halfway there, I realized I had left my container at the well, but I spared no extra running to retrieve it. Telling others about Living Water made a simple water vessel unimportant.

I dared to speak to the elders of Sychar about Jesus, the *Taheb*, the Restorer, the Messiah. I met the looks of gossipy women and, instead, danced in their presence. I grasped the hands of children holding up five fingers, and I laughed. With tears wetting my face and joy permeating my soul, I entreated them, "Come, see a man who told me everything I ever did! Could this man be the Restorer, the Messiah!? He is at the well of Jacob. Come and see!"

One man said, "Is this the woman who never speaks to us? What could have happened to her? Let us go and see." It must have been my sheer excitement, or perhaps the weight of the word "Messiah," but once I sang it out loud, "Come, come and see," many followed me to meet Jesus at the well. Did they follow because they were puzzled by my transformation, or were they just curious?

Jesus stood on the hill near the well, and watched us all approach. Gesturing to the crowd, He said, "Lift up your eyes and look upon the fields. They are white and ready to harvest."

One of the Sychar elders approached Him. He bowed slightly. "This woman has given witness that You know everything about her." He pointed to me. "Something has indeed happened to her. We wish to hear more of Your words."

The Messiah seemed to radiate. After hearing Jesus speak, the elders invited Him to dine tonight in Sychar. He graciously accepted.

This evening Samaritans and a Jew will break bread together. We will share stories of lament and renewal and hope and the kingdom of God for all people—even Samaritans with painful pasts.

No man has ever spoken words like this man. His words feed life; they behold hope; they gush truth. It is hard for me to believe what has taken place today. My story is no longer a rejection tale to mourn, but a beautiful epic to hope for. God has given me another chance.

I am heading to the feast now!

THE SACRED TEXT

Jesus knew the Pharisees had heard that he was baptizing and making more disciples than John (though Jesus himself didn't baptize them—his disciples did). So he left Judea and returned to Galilee.

He had to go through Samaria on the way. Eventually he came to the Samaritan village of Sychar, near the field that Jacob gave to his son Joseph. Jacob's well was there; and Jesus, tired from the long walk, sat wearily beside the well about noontime. Soon a Samaritan woman came to draw water, and Jesus said to her, "Please give me a drink." He was alone at the time because his disciples had gone into the village to buy some food.

The woman was surprised, for Jews refuse to have anything to do with Samaritans. She said to Jesus, "You are a Jew, and I am a Samaritan woman. Why are you asking me for a drink?"

Jesus replied, "If you only knew the gift God has for you and who you are speaking to, you would ask me, and I would give you living water."

"But sir, you don't have a rope or a bucket," she said, "and this well is very deep. Where would you get this living water? And besides, do you think you're greater than our ancestor Jacob, who gave us this well? How can you offer better water than he and his sons and his animals enjoyed?"

Jesus replied, "Anyone who drinks this water will soon become thirsty again. But those who drink the water I give will never be thirsty again. It becomes a fresh, bubbling spring within them, giving them eternal life."

"Please, sir," the woman said, "give me this water! Then I'll never be thirsty again, and I won't have to come here to get water."

"Go and get your husband," Jesus told her.

"I don't have a husband," the woman replied.

Jesus said, "You're right! You don't have a husband—for you have had five husbands, and you aren't even married to the man you're living with now. You certainly spoke the truth!"

"Sir," the woman said, "you must be a prophet. So tell me, why is it that you Jews insist that Jerusalem is the only place of worship, while we Samaritans claim it is here at Mount Gerizim, where our ancestors worshiped?"

Jesus replied, "Believe me, dear woman, the time is coming when it will no longer matter whether you worship the Father on this mountain or in Jerusalem. You Samaritans know very little about the one you worship, while we Jews know all about him, for salvation comes through the Jews. But the time is coming—indeed it's here now—when true worshipers will worship the Father in spirit and in truth. The Father is looking for those who will worship him that way. For God is Spirit, so those who worship him must worship in spirit and in truth."

The woman said, "I know the Messiah is coming—the one who is called Christ. When he comes, he will explain everything to us."

Then Jesus told her, "I Am the Messiah!"

Just then his disciples came back. They were shocked to find him talking to a woman, but none of them had the nerve to ask, "What do you want with her?" or "Why are you talking to her?" The woman left her water jar beside the well and ran back to the village, telling everyone, "Come and see a man who told me everything I ever did! Could he possibly be the Messiah?" So the people came streaming from the village to see him.

Meanwhile, the disciples were urging Jesus, "Rabbi, eat something."

But Jesus replied, "I have a kind of food you know nothing about."

"Did someone bring him food while we were gone?" the disciples asked each other.

Then Jesus explained: "My nourishment comes from doing the will of God, who sent me, and from finishing his work. You know the saying,

'Four months between planting and harvest.' But I say, wake up and look around. The fields are already ripe for harvest. The harvesters are paid good wages, and the fruit they harvest is people brought to eternal life. What joy awaits both the planter and the harvester alike! You know the saying, 'One plants and another harvests.' And it's true. I sent you to harvest where you didn't plant; others had already done the work, and now you will get to gather the harvest."

Many Samaritans from the village believed in Jesus because the woman had said, "He told me everything I ever did!" When they came out to see him, they begged him to stay in their village. So he stayed for two days, long enough for many more to hear his message and believe. Then they said to the woman, "Now we believe, not just because of what you told us, but because we have heard him ourselves. Now we know that he is indeed the Savior of the world."

—John 4:1–42 NLT

WALKING IT OUT

Jesus is full of surprises. He does things that the smartest mortals would never anticipate. The story you just read is a case in point.

Some of the most sublime things that ever came from the lips of the Son of God were uttered to a woman who was a walking scandal and embarrassment.

In fact, the longest personal conversation Jesus ever had (recorded in the Gospels) was with this same woman.

Get a good look at her.

She's known multiple divorces in an era where divorce was regarded to be highly shameful.[3]

She's been used up by men and abused by life.

She was undoubtedly uneducated.

And she's presently living in a sinful situation, rendering her ritually unclean.

That said, there are certain nuances in this story that are routinely missed unless we understand something about first-century culture and the Old Testament.

Three Scandals

Three major scandals punctuate this story.

First, Jewish people hated Samaritans. They viewed Samaritans as the worst kinds of outcasts, half-breeds, worse than Gentiles. A first-century Jewish common saying was, "the daughters of the Samaritans are menstruants from the cradle," meaning they were born unclean.[4]

THE DAY I MET JESUS

So for Jesus, a Jew, to be talking to a Samaritan meant instant scandal.

Second, Jews were not to eat with Samaritans nor share a common cup with them.

Yet Jesus had no qualms with either. He had no objection to drinking the water this woman gave Him, and He had no issue eating with the Samaritans in her village after their encounter that day.

Third, Jewish men were not allowed to speak to women alone in public locations—a strongly held taboo.[5] What is more, since the disciples left to get food, Jesus and this woman sat alone.

For these three reasons, the disciples reacted in shock when they discovered Jesus talking to *this* woman . . . alone in a public place.

But although the Lord clearly violated three religious and cultural norms, He did not seem to care. His chief priority? Fulfilling His Father's will, no matter the cost, despite judgment and even scandal.

A Walking Embarrassment

The ancient Christians named the Samaritan woman Photine (commonly pronounced Foteenie), which means "enlightened one." Regardless of whether this was her real name or not, we'll honor her with the name Photine in this section.[6]

It was no random act that Photine visited the well to draw water alone at noon. The typical time that women drew water was early in the morning or at sunset. And women typically accomplished this tedious work in groups.

So why did Photine visit the well at noon alone? Because of her reputation, the women of Sychar most likely shunned her. She probably grew tired of the scornful stares of the other women in the village. She wearied of whispering tongues and wagging heads. This explains why when she arrived at the well, only Jesus sat there.

We can imagine her carrying the shame of her past and the guilt of her present heavy on her shoulders. Here trudged a woman who loved others, but rarely felt love in return. We can reasonably surmise she was attractive because many Samaritan men had found her desirable. But she may have suffered some kind of emotional trauma in her background, which made it difficult for her to create lasting bonds. Her life became a collage of slammed doors, serial rejections, multiple failures, heartache, and probably abuse.

Most single women were economically marginalized. Thus her desperate situation would have forced her to attach herself to a new man as quickly as possible. She was trapped in a life of immorality and deemed a social outcast. Such rote hopelessness must have diminished her life to eke out a daily existence on autopilot, numb to the world.

A Divine Appointment

Jesus ventured from Judea to Galilee. But He took a route that few Jews normally traveled. The exception was if it was during the Jewish festivals or if they were in a hurry.

The text says "he had to pass through Samaria" (John 4:4 ESV).

We can see no external reason why He had to go through Samaria, so we assume—as John tells us repeatedly—that the Father led Jesus in that direction (John 5:19). The Spirit blows where He wills.

The Father had chosen Photine in Christ before the foundation of the world. And so He led His Son Jesus to share the water of life with her at this specific point in human history.

And now, at this well, a lonely, despised Samaritan meets a lonely, despised Jew.

The root of Photine's loneliness was betrayal and sin, but His loneliness came because of human jealousy (Matt. 27:18; Mark 15:10; John 4:1–3; 12:19). His detractors were envious of Him so they persuaded others to reject Him.

It was high noon, and the sun bled hot.

Jesus was weary and thirsty from the long journey (possibly a six-hour trip), so He sat at the well to rest. No doubt, at the Father's leading.

Understand that for Jesus to ask for a drink was highly unusual. Some scholars believe Photine interpreted the request to be flirtatious. Or perhaps she thought, *You Jews won't give us Samaritans the time of day unless you need something*. But by His request Jesus affirmed her dignity.

Interestingly, when Christ spoke of "living water," Photine thought He was speaking of fresh or flowing water as opposed to stagnant or well water. But as was His custom, Jesus was talking on a spiritual level. The living waters

Jesus referred to were the spiritual waters that flowed from heavenly places. Photine eventually caught on.

A Tale of Two Mountains

When Jesus put His finger on the sore spot of her past and present situation, He wasn't wagging His finger in her face to shame her. He simply revealed that He knew exactly who she was and understood her anguish.

Photine's response that Jesus must be a prophet was striking because Samaritans didn't believe in prophets like Jews did. Samaritans believed no real prophets lived after the death of Moses. Except for the one Prophet they were all anticipating. You see, the Samaritans weren't looking for a political Messiah from the line of David. They were rather waiting for a Prophet *like* Moses who would restore all things. The Samaritans called him the *Taheb*, or Restorer. He was the equivalent of the Jewish Messiah.

Feeling uncomfortable with Jesus' highly personal observations, Photine quickly changed the subject and waxed theological (John 4:18–19). She brought up the theological division over two rival mountains. The Samaritans worshiped on Mount Gerizim and the Jews worshiped on Mount Zion. Samaritans refused to worship in Jerusalem, preferring their own temple built on Mount Gerizim in 400 BC. The Jews didn't recognize Mount Gerizim as a place of worship, and in 128 BC they destroyed the Samaritan temple. This only added to the bitter hostility between the two people groups.

Samaritans practiced circumcision and Sabbath observance, but they only accepted the Pentateuch (the first five books of the Old Testament). They also regarded Israel's history as apostate. They claimed that the true sacred site stood on Mount Gerizim. They rejected the location and validity of the Jewish temple.

Jesus went on to tell Photine that God the Father was turning the tables on how people would worship Him. God now sought *any* person to worship Him in spirit (in reality, not pretense) and truth (according to who He really is) from *any* place—a new era with a new kind of worship.

Such an idea was revolutionary to first-century Jews and Samaritans.

When Photine moved on from the subject, suggesting that one day the Restorer will come and sort all of these worship controversies out, Jesus stunned her by saying, "The person you are speaking to right now is the Messiah!"

The marvel of the story is that when He uttered those words, she actually believed Him. The Messiah of the Jews and the *Taheb* of the Samaritans, God's representative on earth, was a Jew! And even though He knew her shameful past and her sinful present, He offered her living water.

Photine had never seen just gentleness in a man. No criticism, no condemnation, no anger. She had known the sting of racism and prejudice from Jews all her life, yet she received none from Jesus.

What a Lord!

During their conversation, the disciples returned, bearing food in their hands. They were stunned to find Jesus talking with a Samaritan woman, and were hesitant to ask Him about it.

But Photine was so transformed by the encounter that she rushed to tell the elders of Sychar about this man. Utterly preoccupied, she abandoned her water pot. She left the bringing of water to her home for the bringing of men to Jesus. The insignificance of her life had been swallowed up by the significance of the man she just met.

Transformation

This was perhaps the first time Photine could hold her head high and look squarely into the eyes of the city elders.

One wonders why the elders believed her report. Perhaps because she had never spoken to them or the townspeople before, they couldn't help but take her seriously. She must have spoken with pride and wonder about the unusual prophet she had just met—delivering her message with unflinching boldness.

Samaritans didn't value the testimony of a woman any more than Jews did . . . especially a woman with a reputation like Photine's. Yet her passionate exuberance seemed to sway them.

But once they encountered Jesus for themselves, the elders no longer depended on her testimony. They did not denigrate her witness, but merely confirmed it. So impressed with the young prophet, they urged Him to stay in Sychar. Because of their insistence, Jesus accepted and stayed in the Samaritan village for two days. And through

His words, many more Samaritans became followers of the true Christ.

There He is. Jesus in Samaria: Eating their food, using their utensils, and teaching them . . . things that Jews are forbidden to do with Samaritans. (When John says, "For Jews have no dealings with Samaritans" in John 4:9 [ESV], he is especially referring to the fact that Jews and Samaritans did not share the same utensils or other instruments.)

Unfortunately, we have no record of what Jesus taught them. But consider the possibility that He spoke about Himself as the bridegroom from heaven (as He had before) with His followers from all tribes, tongues, and nations as His bride.

If so, they would have made a connection with the writings of Moses and their father Jacob. You see, Moses, Isaac, and Jacob all met their brides at wells.[7]

When Jacob met his bride Rachel at a well, it was noontime!

Once again, John paints Jesus to be the new Jacob. (John already unveiled Jesus as the new Jacob in the "stairway to heaven" dialogue that Jesus had with Nathanael. Compare John 1:51 with Genesis 28:12ff.) In John 3, Jesus is presented as the bridegroom. In this passage in John 4, we have an image of the bride in the Samaritan woman; she is half Jew and half Gentile, the same makeup as the bride and body of Christ (Eph. 2:14–16; 5:25–33).

Here stood a despised and desperate woman. Thrice an outcast in Jewish thought. An unclean Samaritan. A woman who had been with five different husbands. And a woman with a sixth man who didn't wish to marry her.

But on that special day, the seventh man arrived. And He would turn out to be the Messiah. Not the national leader of the old Israel, but the *Taheb*, the Restorer, "the Savior of the entire world" (as they called Him).

Yes, on that day, salvation ventured outside of Judaism into the Gentile world. Once again, we see Jesus doing what He does best: touching and transforming the unclean and crossing boundaries of culture, social status, and gender. The Jesus of the Gospels is more concerned with people than the traditions that separate them. And His scandalous behavior pointed to the new reality of the unity of the Spirit and the global nature of God's salvation.

After six failed relationships, Photine encountered her true husband. A man who would love her like no other man ever had. A man who would never use or abuse her, but who would cherish her with the purest love in the universe. And she, a woman of ill repute, became the first evangelist to the Samaritans.

That day the Samaritan community not only met their Messiah, they met their bridegroom . . . the lover of their souls.

What a Christ!

Consider this, dear reader. If your Lord could love an insignificant, uneducated, "worthless," sinful Samaritan . . . a multiple divorcee . . . an outcast among her own people, then you can rest assured He loves and accepts you too.

Why? Because if you have bowed the knee to His lordship and trusted in His saviorhood, then you are also part of His lovely bride.

But there's more. Note Jesus' words: "He who drinks from this well will thirst again."

Living Water Today

Can you relate to this woman? If you've ever been lonely, if you've ever known use or abuse, if you've ever experienced the wearisome burden of carrying your sins, with all of the shame and guilt that accompanies them, then certainly you can.

Jesus told this woman that drinking from Jacob's well would eventually leave her thirsty (John 4:13). In the same way, the wells of this world will always run dry . . . eventually. A cup of water may satisfy your thirst for a short time, but soon enough, you will thirst again.

Fame can satisfy for a time. Fortune can satisfy for a time. The pleasures of sin are indeed satisfying . . . for a season (Heb 11:25).

But eventually, you will thirst again.

Not so with the water that Jesus Christ offers to us. In fact, Jesus Christ Himself is that water. He is the Spring of living water, the well of eternal life which can be received and enjoyed *now* (Rev. 22:1; 7:17; 21:6). God Himself is living water (Jer. 2:13; 17:13).

All who partake of that real water—which is Christ—will never thirst again.

And what is needed to partake of this water? To open your heart, receive, and drink.

> For in one Spirit we were all baptized into one body—Jews or Greeks, slaves or free—and all were made to drink of one Spirit. (1 Cor. 12:13 ESV)

> My people have committed two sins:
> They have forsaken me,
>   the spring of living water,
> and have dug their own cisterns,
>   broken cisterns that cannot hold water. (Jer. 2:13)

This water is "the gift of God." You can't buy it; it's sheer gift. You simply must receive its life-giving qualities. Jesus Christ, the lonely despised artisan, the one called a bastard, a traitor to Rome, an accused false prophet, and a deceiver of the people, is the beautiful gift of God. He is the living water that never runs dry.

Sadly, Christians so often turn to every other thing, digging in their own strength. And even when they create cisterns to hold stagnant (non-living) water, the cisterns eventually break and cannot even hold the stagnant water.

Choose the real water of heaven and you will never thirst again.

The Aftermath in Acts

Six years later, a Jewish man named Philip, a disciple of the Messiah, visited Samaria and proclaimed the Good News. He announced that the Messiah had died, had been buried, and had risen again on the third day. And He was now a life-giving Spirit to live in all who trust in Him—making them part of His beloved bride (1 Cor. 15:45).[8]

It's likely that the Samaritan woman was present when Philip preached the gospel in Samaria. She had already met the living water in Person years before. Now she was drinking that living water—the very thing that Jesus had said He would provide six years earlier if she simply asked.

Not long after, Peter and John visit Samaria. And they probably remember this woman after meeting her. Perhaps she tells John the full story of how she met Jesus at Jacob's well and the conversation that ensued. And John will write the account in the Gospel that bears his name. (Note that only Jesus and the woman knew about the conversation since the apostles weren't present. So we assume that she recounted the whole story to John.) Listen to the story of the gospel preached in Samaria, and if you listen carefully, you can hear the story of this Samaritan woman too:

> But the believers who were scattered preached the Good News about Jesus wherever they went. Philip, for example, went to the city of Samaria and told the people there about the Messiah. Crowds listened intently to Philip because they were eager to hear his message and see the miraculous signs he did. Many evil spirits were cast out, screaming as they left their victims. And many who had been paralyzed or lame were healed. So there was great joy in that city.
>
> A man named Simon had been a sorcerer there for many years, amazing the people of Samaria and claiming to be someone great. Everyone, from the least to the greatest, often spoke of him as "the Great One—the Power of God." They listened

closely to him because for a long time he had astounded them with his magic.

But now the people believed Philip's message of Good News concerning the Kingdom of God and the name of Jesus Christ. As a result, many men and women were baptized. Then Simon himself believed and was baptized. He began following Philip wherever he went, and he was amazed by the signs and great miracles Philip performed.

When the apostles in Jerusalem heard that the people of Samaria had accepted God's message, they sent Peter and John there. As soon as they arrived, they prayed for these new believers to receive the Holy Spirit. The Holy Spirit had not yet come upon any of them, for they had only been baptized in the name of the Lord Jesus. Then Peter and John laid their hands upon these believers, and they received the Holy Spirit. (Acts 8:4–17 NLT)

An Ode to the Desperate Samaritan Woman

To summarize this chapter, we offer this poem that says it all with poetic beauty:

> I am a woman
> Of no distinction
> Of little importance
> I am a woman of no reputation save that which is bad
> You whisper as I pass by and
> Cast judgmental glances
> Though you don't really take the time to look at me
> Or even get to know me
>
> For to be known is to be loved
> And to be loved is to be known
> And otherwise what's the point in doing either one of them
>   in the first place?

I want to be known
I want someone to look at my face and not just see
Two eyes a nose a mouth and two ears
But to see all that I am and could be
All my hopes loves and fears
That's too much to hope for
To wish for
Or pray for
So I don't
Not anymore
Now I keep to myself, and by that I mean
The pain that keeps me in my own private jail
The pain that's brought me here
At midday
To this well

To ask for a drink is no big request but to ask it of me
A woman
Unclean
Ashamed
Used and abused
An outcast
A failure
A disappointment
A sinner
No drink passing from these hands to Your lips could ever
    be refreshing
Only condemning
As I am sure You condemn me now
But You don't

You're a man of no distinction
Though of the utmost importance
A man with little reputation at least so far
You whisper and tell me to my face

What all those glances have been about and You take the
    time
To really look at me

But You don't need to get to know me
For to be known is to be loved and
To be loved is to be known
And You know me; You actually know me
All of me and everything about me
Every thought inside and hair on top of my head
Every hurt stored up
Every hope, every dread
My past and my future
All I am and could be
You tell me everything
You tell me about me

And that which is spoken by another
Would bring hate and condemnation
Coming from You brings love grace mercy hope and
    salvation
I've heard of One to come that would save a wretch like me
And here in my presence you say
I am He

To be known is to be loved and
To be loved is to be known
And I just met You, but I love You
I don't know You but I want to
Let me run back to town
This is way too much for just me
There are others
Brothers, sisters, lovers, haters
The good and the bad
Sinners and saints

Who should hear what You've told me
Who should see what You've showed me
Who should taste what You gave me
Who should feel how You forgave me

For to be known is to be loved and to be loved is to be
    known
And they all need this too
We all do
Need it for our own[9]

The story of Jesus and His telling conversation with a desperate Samaritan woman teaches us so many things. But perhaps most of all, it teaches us that despite our greatest and most severe sins, the Lord of glory cherishes us.

You, dear Christian, are not outside of God's gracious reach. We serve a Lord who searches for us and makes divine appointments to pursue us. And in His merciful eyes, regardless of our past, we—His image-bearers—are worth being pursued.

As Photine exuberantly told her neighbors, "Come and see" (John 4:29 NLT), we invite you to do the same. *Come and see that the Lord is good.*

4

Diary of a Woman with a Flow of Blood

Dearest Talitha,

I am having these words scribed because you asked me the question again today, and I want you to know the whole story, not rumors, not snippets, but its entirety. Would you please be a caretaker of these feeble words? Not to publish them or shout them from Judean rooftops, but to coddle them close to your sweet heart, as Jesus' mother treasured memories of her Son in the recesses of her soul.

My eyes dim this dusky evening, but my heart brims with life in light of you who twirled before me under the wide smile of the sun, all blessedly twelve years old. Laughing. Breathless. A pretty jewel of a granddaughter, unaware of life's tainting, you are. You have become a token of a terrible but poignant memory, of a twelve-year exile from the land of the living. You have danced this earth as long as I trudged it, untouchable.

But now, what remains of life pelts me as sundown threatens to fade my story to shadows. I fight against dim eyes and the inevitability of heaven beyond the grave. I cannot help but revel in what He did thirty-two years ago. All this for a woman who thought the flow of blood would steal her to afterlife much, much sooner.

The story I am telling you sensationalized my village at first. Did you know people called me Veronica the Miraculous, once dead, now alive? Perhaps this fame caught your *zayde*'s attention.[1] Whatever the reason, I am grateful for his knowing look, though I mourn its loss. His sad but familiar absence thickened my tongue this afternoon when you suddenly stopped whirling. You sat on the dirt breathless and said, "Why is there no *zayde* for me, *Bubbe*?"[2]

"He has adventured before us, dear Talitha. Right now he dances on golden streets, warming them up for us." I tried to say the words without quavering, but you who shared my empathetic bent knew my broken heart threatened tears.

You stood in a fluid moment and sat gently on my lap. You stroked my gray hair, now hanging free.

"You know what he told me before he died?"

"No, tell me, *Bubbe*," you said.

"He said the first thing he would do is thank Jesus for healing me so many years ago. Can you imagine that?"

You nodded, though you never had the pleasure of knowing his dancing eyes, quick wit, or supreme affection for me. You yawped your way into the world six Sabbaths after he left it.

I let a tear loose, then another.

"I think you are so very beautiful, *Bubbe*," you told me. Remember how you touched one of my tears? "Even when you leak," you said.

And I laughed then, throaty, which sent me into spasmodic coughs. Were you afraid then? You dutifully fetched a cup of water, brought it to my lips, but I had to push it away. My lungs screamed for air, and my heaves could not seem to grab at it. You patted my back, then broke into tender prayer. And as you said the name of Jesus, my coughing stopped. Even now, His name sets things aright.

You held my hand, looked at me with those big hazel eyes. "Will you not tell me the whole story, *Bubbe*, about what it was like before Jesus made everything better?"

I drank a sip of water, remembering the years of tasting copper on my tongue, how frail I had become, how marked I felt by my infirmity, how I grew accustomed to loneliness. Some of the memories have faded like old cloth hanging too long in the sun, and I had to fight to recall what I wore the day I met Jesus. "I will tell you tomorrow," I told you.

And yet after you left to make dinner alongside your mama, and as I tried to steady my breathing, I realized we are not guaranteed tomorrow, are we? As my chest rattle deepens, I owe you the story written plain, best as I can recall, before the sun stoops beneath the mountains.

Did you know I was your age when the bleeding began? Just as it did for women since the dawn of Eve. I welcomed the flow of pomegranate red, knowing my life would change for the better because of it. I remember saying, "Mama, it is my time."

She smiled wearily. "Yes, it is." She touched my face and looked at me with sad eyes. "You are becoming a woman—a *niddah*." She followed her words with instructions from the Torah about uncleanness and how I needed to be careful not to touch others when this issue of blood made its monthly habit. Your mama will have this talk with you, Talitha, or perhaps she already has?

But somehow my flow of blood never took a Sabbath. Nearly every day it came. Some days the flow was so heavy, I fainted, and when I awoke, blinking at the sun above, I trembled with questions. Would I bleed to death? Why was this happening to me? Mother would lift me to my feet then, sigh heavily as if she carried an unseen burden, and whisper a prayer heavenward. Every time she did that, my fear grew. Did she know something I did not?

I began to believe I would die because of the constant, nagging bleeding, but I kept this terror to myself because there were practical matters to attend to. With no time between bouts of bleeding to ritually cleanse myself before another bout assaulted me, I had to learn to live without touching another human being, worrying I would nullify each person's ability to worship.

Like you, Talitha, I loved to pray. I told the Almighty my petitions, but His ears seemed closed to my plight. I wanted to be so near to God I could hear His heartbeat, but I could never enter His glorious presence, even on the outskirts of the temple. Certainly not the court of Israel, when blood flowed fresh and women were not permitted. Not the women's court either. My perpetual state prohibited me from worship.

Sometimes I would steal away at night and climb the hills nearby. A little older than you, I believed if I neared the sky, God would reach down and rescue me. I thought He could hear me better if I yelled from the heights.

But the bleeding continued. Week upon week. Month stretched to month. Year upon year. No longer *niddah*, a menstruating woman, I became *zavah*, a woman perpetually unclean. I pray that you never have to experience this trauma, dear Talitha.

Mama promised this would cease when I married. That once a man became one with me, my bleeding would dry up for nine months, the sweet reward being a baby swaddling near my breast. With Jorim, this became my hope. He was not your *zayde*, child. I hope you are not shocked to know I knew a man before your grandfather.

On the few days I did not bleed, we met as married people do, only to have the specter haunt again. My bleeding continued. No babies yawped their way into this world. My husband had to keep a separate home.

Everything I sat upon, everything I touched, everywhere I traveled became ceremonially unclean. I was a leper with no leprosy. One who committed manslaughter with no City of Refuge in which to escape. An exile with no true nation.

Jorim cried the day the Certificate of Divorce sat between us on the wooden table he had crafted. The tears wet his beard, and they flowed as effusively as my own trail of blood. "You are my wife," he said. "My wife." As if he could say the phrase one thousand more times, he could force our lives to work with two simple words. But he could not stop the inevitable. This story could not have a happy ending.

I belonged to Jorim four Passovers, and he to me. I loved him enough to beg for the divorce, to force his hand, if only to give him a better life—with a wife whose womb would carry on his family's name. He deserved a perfect woman such as that. And not long after he would find her in Yohanna.

"This is how it must be." I said these words to God, but I could not meet Jorim's eyes just then. My body had betrayed us all—and all suffered because of it. My fault. My blood. My problem. "I am determined to heal," I said, but the words seemed to be swallowed up in our grief.

Jorim held my hands in his. "You are beautiful." With this, his voice hitched. And my heart died inside me. I had obeyed God; we had honored Him by trying to be fruitful and multiply—and yet God had not answered my pleas for a quiver full of children. And now, divorce.

Alone and desperate to heal, I spent much time with doctors, most who stole more from me than denarii. They revoked my dignity. One accused me of unconfessed sin. Another told me to simply have more faith, to pray more petitions. Another blamed me, saying blood and barrenness were God's judgment upon my kind. Another said the flow of blood came from prostitution—a ridiculous claim.

Watching you dance today as the sun winked on you contrasted starkly with my life back then. Even walking became my burden. Just to draw water seventy paces away took my entire daily effort. Can you imagine that, Talitha? My heart fluttered constantly. My breath came in short wisps as it does now, but I was only twenty-four years old. My eyes dizzied even more than they blur today in my convalescence.

As I plodded one tortured step after another, I begged God to have mercy on me and take my life. (I am sorry for this, Talitha. I had so little faith then, and my God felt so small, tinier than an ant in those days.) In my darkest, quietest, lonely moments, I flailed between believing God had a plan for this malady, like He redeemed Job's terrible lot, and letting go of all belief that God even loved me. Eventually I pitched my tent in the latter camp, letting bitterness take its terrible root.

No hope.

Only disease.

Loneliness.

Poverty.

Betrayed by the Law I love.

And then, despair.

Talitha, I pray you never have to know the darkness that hovered over me in those days. I pray you dance throughout your life, connected to others, loved by many.

I must have cried over four thousand days, but the effort to wail sapped the energy I needed to live, so I had to fast tears. The Almighty collected them in a bottle, as the psalmist wrote, which must, for me, be as large as the stone vessel flanking your home. So many tears.

As my words are being scribed, I remember one particular moonlit night when my thoughts crazed through me. Funny how you think your memory has faded to dust, only to have moments scream back. Perhaps it is the sheer act of wanting to leave you a legacy of my story, or maybe it is the hand of God moving my mind to remember. It could be both.

That night God seemed to speak to me on the quietness of my sleeping mat. Under blinking stars the breeze lightly kicked up, and His voice whispered through me. Was it not unlike when Elijah heard the voice of God? Not in rushing, tree-bending wind. Not as the earth gave way with a quake. Not as fire raged. But in a still, quiet voice. Talitha, I wish you could have been there to hear such a wonder.

You will see My glory. Do not lose faith.

I nursed those words to my heart, but then hope waned and I wondered if the voice I heard was my own wishful thinking. All that to say, dear Talitha, do not doubt the voice of God like I did. If you hear it, and you know in the moment that it is His whispers, make a choice not to lose faith. Remember those words. Repeat them to yourself in the cadence of a psalm. Even if the world pelts you with accusation or faith-stealing circumstances, choose to rest in the knowing that He has spoken.

After twelve years of bleeding, I fixed my thoughts on death as my life flowed from me like a stream. I lived dizzy, and my tongue stuck thick in my mouth. I tried to picture my Jorim, but the haze of years obscured his face. On the outskirts of life, sometimes I thought I would see him standing with his new wife Yohanna, but I was never sure if it was him or an illusion or a man of similar bones. Or maybe just a mirage.

As a young girl, Mama called me a chirping bird. I would chatter my way through life, speaking to young and old, infirm and healthy. I seemed to have an insatiable curiosity about people. You see, Talitha? We are kindred that way. Because of my fascination, I begged for information, asking question upon question. One time Mama reprimanded me for asking the elderly Esther why she grew a beard on her chin. But the old lady smiled, toothless, and patted my head. "The Good Lord saw fit to help me understand a man," she said. And then cackled her way home.

Because of my blood, I could no longer interact with people. Instead, I sat alongside the byways of life and watched others live their blessed lives before me. I invented stories for them, entire histories. A hunched-over man? He possessed a wicked sense of humor, and spent his days in carpentry, though he loved wine more than he loved his family. That woman? She cared for orphans with a joyful wink and a secret agony-desire to be a mother herself—so much like me.

Perhaps you will invent stories too, Talitha?

Besides my silent storytelling, I forced myself to listen to the cadence of conversation. Faceless to everyone, I blended into the scenery, so I became privy to secrets, shames, and joys.

I heard the rumors about this man, Jesus, who crossed invisible boundaries and touched the unclean, the demonized, the broken. Some called Him a miracle man. Others, a prophet. Some spewed that He was a demon troublemaker, intent on overthrowing our entire way of life—a lawbreaker.

But it was His healing touch I locked my ears on. This man healed people. Even the blind.

Talitha, what I am going to tell you next is the truth. And I suppose it would be easy for you to believe because I am still alive writing this, and I have told bits and pieces of this story before. Even so, it is a fantastical story, but all true.

Jesus arrived by boat in Capernaum—so close that meeting Him became a possibility. But my legs refused to obey. I forced myself to pull up from my stained sleeping mat, commanding my legs to dance like Ezekiel's dry bones, but they did not obey. Blood continued its steady, relentless, awful stream from my womb, but it refused to invigorate my legs.

I do not know why, but I believed with every ounce of life left in me that Jesus could heal me. Perhaps this had been God's promise under the moonlight? The same kind of self-mustering came with every doctor visit, only to leave me broke and broken. But this anticipation felt different—way down deep in my tired bones.

So I knelt.

Then I pulled to standing on my walking stick, still wrenched by pain. The blood continued its menacing stream down my legs. I told myself that the only way to see Jesus was to walk through the crowds, something I could not do because of my uncleanness. If anyone recognized me, women would pull their children away with looks of horror on their faces, and someone would muscle me away to the byways. So I made sure my head and face were covered so no one would notice who I was.

Oh dear Talitha, I pray you never have to know this exile, though now I am grateful for the twelve lonely years because it has made me so very aware of the pain in people's eyes. My blessing for you is that you will know how to serve the broken without having to be broken first. Dare to ask for people's stories, no matter how downcast their eyes may be.

But back to the day. The crowds swarmed around me, Talitha, far more than the market day you and I are accustomed to. They pressed in, shouting, trying to herald the attention of Jesus. Words flew overhead about Jairus, an important man, who had asked Jesus to please heal his daughter. I guessed that was where Jesus walked—toward the man's home.

I moved through the crowd, quieting my breaths, trying not to grunt with each step. It would be impossible, but I was seized by this thought: *If I only touch His garments, I shall be restored to health.*

If only. I took one step through the peopled crowd. Then another.

I could touch. Families bustled around me, not realizing they touched a person who would render them unclean. Still, I pressed on, praying that I could make this journey without notice. My heart pounded in my throat. I stopped. Pulled in a breath. Instructed my eyes to quit tilting the world to the left, then right. The world spun, and my vision narrowed.

His garments. I told myself to take another step, despite the whirling world. I only needed to sneak my way toward the tassel at the edges of His cloak, nothing more—certainly not His hand, His forearm, His shoulder. Too risky.

I knew I would die anyway. This touch would be my last hopeless act, this reaching for one small tassel . . .

I shall. Dust scurried around Jesus as people plodded and chattered and preened to make their impressions. So many demanded something from Him. They shouted their stories of woe. I remembered the words I had cherished: *You will see My glory. Do not lose faith.* And I tried to believe them, Talitha. You see how small my faith was? Smaller than a mustard seed.

Be restored. Jairus' daughter neared death, according to the whispers around me. I uttered a prayer for her, for the man's family.

To health. My feet kept their tortured plodding, my heart continued its beat, my breath coming in spurts and sputters, much as it does now as I dictate these words. I so wanted to be whole that I could not help but keep moving toward Jesus. He would not have to see me. Touching a mere tassel would not inconvenience a soul. Even so, even though it might defile Him, I thought this would be less corrupting than to touch Him directly. I wavered between worry about this and justification that clothing was not exactly the same as flesh.

Jesus would be the last healer for which I would risk my pride. My legs gave out beneath me, just a few paces away from Him, but He kept walking. I crawled on skinned and bruised knees, death nearing. Perhaps I would die here in the crowd, finally surrounded by people. Maybe this would become God's sweet blessing for me, a people-loving woman, to die among the ones who outcast her.

But Jesus loomed close. I feared I left a trail of blood beneath me, but I was grateful the crowd trampled the evidence underfoot, covering my defilement in the dust. I pulled my body nearer, stretching. Within grasp. I stretched my arm toward His humble cloak, but He stepped away again. I dropped my head to the ground, kissing the dust, the world tumbling around me. My vision narrowed again, and stars blurred my vision.

I would die there.

The ground felt like feathers, willing me to succumb to it, to give up trying, to sleep forever.

No.

No.

I cannot describe how *no* echoed through me, but it felt like a trumpet blast, a summoning like Jericho's trumpets before the broken walls.

I forced myself to open my eyes. Jesus stood a few paces ahead, and though the crowd pressed around Him, I discerned a straight, narrow path toward Him. So I forced myself to crawl. I drug my bleeding body to Him in one agonizing urge.

I tottered to standing.

I stretched toward His cloak.

And touched one tassel.

The flow of blood that had become my terrible companion as many years as you have lived, Talitha, instantly ceased. The weakness in my limbs disappeared. The fuzzy thinking I had for hundreds of Sabbaths, clarified. My skin felt supple. My tongue returned to normal size. My desire to eat dirt to fill some insatiable hunger shifted. You'll find this funny, Talitha, but I wanted to eat a pomegranate. Remember how we share them together now, one seed at a time while our hands drip red?

Jesus stopped. Turned around and asked, "Who touched My robe?"

All the joy I felt drained from me. He noticed me. I had contaminated Jesus, and now He would chastise me for my sin. I trembled both within and without, shaking so violently I could not calm myself. I looked away, a bird caught in a fowler, wanting an escape route, but the crowd prevented me. They seemed to relish this terrible confrontation as they formed a menacing circle around me. Or maybe I imagined all this.

"Look at this crowd pressing around You," one of Jesus' companions said. "How can you ask, 'Who touched Me?'"

I let out my breath. A diversion. So many had touched the Teacher. I was one of many. I stood on steady legs, then tried to flee.

Jesus looked throughout the crowd, left and right, meeting people's eyes. "I know someone touched Me because I sensed power leaving Me."

Even as I wanted to skulk away, I could not tear myself away from those words.

And then Jesus looked right at me, Talitha. In that holy instant He knew my secret. I had touched His robe. He knew. And I knew He knew.

I could do nothing but tremble, then move toward Him, my new body lunging so quickly it surprised me. I fell to my knees in front of Jesus. For the first time I did not worry about the crowd, about being unclean.

My words started hesitant and halted, but then rushed from me. "I have been unclean many years," I told Him. I recounted the twelve-year story I just wrote to you. The bleeding. The doctors. The barrenness. The divorce I insisted upon. My destitute state. The loneliness of exile. My anger at God. It poured from me like water from a vessel, and as it flowed, I felt my weary soul healing. Why would Jesus take such tender time listening to me? I expected a reprimand. A proverb of condemnation.

What I received? Grace. Dignity.

The crowd of people around me cheered at my story, clapping hands and gasping astonishment at this miracle. A strange welcome from those who once thought me unhuman. I did see some people recoil after realizing they may have touched me in the crowd during my unclean state.

But the real miracle to me, Talitha, was the smile of Jesus. He gave me a knowing look, as if He had walked the entire journey with me, felt every sting of pain, regret, fear, weakness, and loneliness. In that moment, He stepped into the story I write now, bled my blood, experienced my exclusion.

Jesus cleared His throat, as if He had been choked up, and said, "Daughter, your faith has made you well. Go in peace. Your suffering is over."

With "daughter" hovering in the air between us, I knew His words about suffering were true. What would life be like from this moment forward? How would I live free from pain?

You will see My glory. Do not lose faith.

Dear Talitha, those words meant for me are also meant for you. Live your life so blessedly free. Dance your dance. Empathize with the hurting, because everyone has a sad story tucked away somewhere. You are a manifestation of the Almighty's *shekinah* glory, sparkling under the sun, so very shimmering and alive. You reflect God's very best on this earth, you perfect girl.

And will you remember me, your *Bubbe*?

When the sun tickles your face and you laugh with your grandchildren as I have laughed with you, throw a kiss skyward, and I will wink down on you, my precious, precious girl. Do not worry a moment about me when you see my lifeless form on my bed. I have lived a stolen life, given to me by the Author of Life. And now I will dance and twirl like you with Jesus on golden streets. But oh will I miss you, dear one.

Your *Bubbe*.

THE SACRED TEXT

Then a woman who had suffered for twelve years from a hemorrhage heard about Jesus and came up in the throng behind him. This woman had suffered a great deal at the hands of doctors, yet none of them could cure her. She had spent all she had and still was no better. In fact, she had only become worse. She touched the hem of Jesus' robe because she told herself, "If only I can touch his clothes, I'll be healed." Instantly the bleeding stopped, and she could feel that she had been cured.

At the same moment Jesus sensed that power had gone out from him. He turned around and said, "Who was touching me? Who touched my clothing?"

Everyone denied it. Peter and the disciples who were with him said, "Master, you can see this huge crowd surrounding you—and yet you ask, 'Who touched me?'"

"I know someone touched me," Jesus answered, "because I sensed power leaving me." He began looking at the crowd to see who had done this.

When the woman realized what had happened to her and saw that she couldn't hide, she came to Jesus, frightened and trembling. She fell down before him and told him all the truth. She explained in front of everyone why she had touched him and how she was instantly healed.

Jesus said to her, "Take heart, daughter. Your faith has saved you. Go in peace, and be free from this affliction."

While he was still speaking, some men from the synagogue leader's home arrived and said to the man [Jairus], "Your daughter has died. Don't bother the teacher anymore."[3]

—See Matthew 9:18–22; Mark 5:25–35; Luke 8:42–49

WALKING IT OUT

Like the other narratives you've read in this book, there's a lot more to this story than meets the eye. So before we make practical application to your life, let's go back in time. Jesus of Nazareth is around nineteen years old. He's an artisan by trade, working with wood and stone. He has not yet commenced ministry.

Near Capernaum lives a man named Jairus. Jairus will one day become the synagogue president of his city—a prestigious position. Jairus becomes father to a baby girl.

Around the same time, in another city, a young woman is stricken with a chronic bleeding problem. The condition will devastate her life.

Fast forward twelve years.

Jesus is thirty-one years old. His ministry is in full gear. He travels from town to town, preaching the good news of the kingdom and healing the sick.

Jairus' daughter is now twelve years old, and she is deathly ill.

At the same time, the woman's chronic bleeding has grown worse.

Her flow of blood has continued for twelve long years. The present life-span of Jairus' daughter.

Jairus and the young woman will meet Jesus of Nazareth. And their lives will forever change.[4]

The primitive church, feeling the woman with the flow of blood deserved a name, called her Veronica. And they alleged that she was from Caesarea Philippi. That may or may not be true. But to honor her memory, we'll call her Veronica in this section.

Unimaginable Desperation

Jairus was a "somebody"—a synagogue official, a prominent figure in first-century Jewish society.

Veronica, however, is a "nobody." She has no remarkable status or occupation.

When Mark recounts Veronica's story, he puts doctors in an unfavorable light, saying that "she had suffered a great deal under the care of many doctors" (5:26).

But when Luke told the story, he omitted this point and remarked that her disease was incurable. Luke, of course, was a physician (Col. 4:14). So he had a more favorable take on his profession.[5]

Some English translations use the word *hemorrhage* to translate the Greek word for Veronica's condition, but this isn't the most accurate English word to describe it. Mark uses the phrase *ousa en rhusei haimatos*, meaning "being in a state of blood flow." Veronica had a steady ooze of blood. Or as the King James puts it, "an issue of blood." Gynecologists today would call it *menometrorrhagia*: heavy, irregular, and unpredictable menstrual periods.

Because regular cyclic menstrual bleeding is the sign of regular ovulation (a prerequisite for conception), Veronica was most probably infertile. So she wouldn't have been pregnant during her twelve-year stretch of menstrual bleeding. This, no doubt, led to a divorce if she was married. In first-century Palestine, a woman's infertility was grounds for a husband to divorce. Further, if Veronica's husband was a righteous man, he could not touch her and remain ritually clean.

Her vaginal bleeding made her ceremonially unclean (Lev. 15:25ff.) and her uncleanness was communicable to others by mere touch (Lev. 15:27ff.). In addition, everything she sat on or touched was also unclean. And during Jesus' day, the rules of ritual purity were growing tighter, not looser.

Add to this, Veronica was most likely anemic from her bleeding, especially given that first-century Palestine had an iron-poor diet. The irregular bleeder was considered a *zavah*, rather than a *niddah*, which meant that she was impure not only during her bleeding, but also for a week after each bleeding episode.

Following each time she bled, she had to make offerings through a priest to cleanse her unclean discharge (Lev. 15:25–28). Consequently, for Veronica to have near-constant bleeding for twelve years in a society like first-century Palestine meant she would live ostracized because she was constantly unclean. Those who knew about her condition wouldn't receive her.

Imagine her life.

Not being able to be touched by another human being.

No embraces.

No affection.

No intimacy.

Ostracism from every worship service.

All for twelve agonizing years.

But beyond that, she neared impoverishment, having spent all her resources on doctors. Add to this, infertility—a terrible shame in first-century Palestine indicating God's judgment in the minds of many. The stigma of childlessness, the stigma of divorce, and the stigma of being perpetually unclean proved unbearable.

All of this explains why she was beyond desperate to find Jesus after she heard about Him. It also explains why she was mortified when, after stealthily touching Jesus' garment, she tried to hide when Jesus asked, "Who touched me?" Mark underscores the point saying that she "came in fear and trembling." Here she was, an unclean woman touching a holy man and thus rendering Him unclean too.

Yet people like Veronica are just the kinds of folks whom Jesus likes to specialize in helping.

Faith vs. God's Power

Veronica's dire situation changed when she "heard the reports about Jesus" (Mark 5:27 ESV).

Recall Paul's words in Romans: "Faith comes by hearing, and hearing by the word of God" (10:17 NKJV).[6]

The reports about Jesus kindled faith in Veronica's heart. Somehow, she knew that if she could simply touch Jesus' garment, she'd be healed. So in an act of scandalous faith, that's precisely what she did.

Some scholars think this indicates that she was superstitious, that touching Jesus' clothes had magical attributes. But we don't think so. Seizing the edge of someone's robe was a gesture of fervent entreaty in Eastern culture. And knowing that she would defile Jesus by touching Him, she probably rationalized in her mind that touching His garment was less severe a ritual violation and she could walk away undetected.

Note that Veronica didn't actually touch the bottom hem of Jesus' garment near His sandals, for it was too far to reach amid such a crowd. She would have been crushed. The word for "hem" or "edge" in Luke is *kraspedon*, and it refers to the ritual tassels commanded by Numbers 15:38–39 and Deuteronomy 22:12.

So she touched the tassel on the end of the square garment thrown over Jesus' left shoulder that hung down the back. (The tassels were reminders to observant Jews of God's commandments.)

The authenticity of Veronica's faith is revealed by the fact that she risked something to touch Jesus. Her "touch" came at a price. She'd be defiling a holy man. She'd also be corrupting every person she rubbed against in the crowd.

It is not without significance that Jesus allowed an unclean woman to touch Him without any consequences to her. It once again shows us the nature of our Lord.

Point: the One who touched lepers and dead bodies wasn't afraid of getting His holy hands dirty with the problems of this fallen world.

Interestingly, Jesus attributes Veronica's healing to two things:

1. The power of God (Mark 5:30).
2. Veronica's faith (Mark 5:34).

Strikingly, Jesus couldn't do any miracles in His hometown Nazareth because of the heavy atmosphere of unbelief there (Mark 6:5).

Contrary to popular conception, faith isn't something mental. It's not hope, hype, wishful thinking, or natural expectation. Faith is a specific kind of trust in God that's built on an internal knowing. This is why Paul writes, "Faith comes by hearing, and hearing by the word of God." Faith is the channel by which Jesus' power can operate.

For this reason, Jesus attributed healings and miracles to a person's faith on the one hand (e.g., Mark 10:52; Luke 7:50; 8:12, 48; 17:19; 18:42; Acts 15:11) and to God's power on the other (Luke 5:17; 8:46).

Daughter of the King

Veronica's act of faith stopped Jesus cold, provoking Him to keep asking, "Who touched Me?" He clearly wanted to draw her out and have her bear witness to the healing she received.

Significantly, Veronica was the only woman whom Jesus ever addressed by the name "Daughter."[7]

Why would He call her daughter? Could it be that the Father spoke through His Son, as He often did? This woman had been destined before the foundation of the world to be a child of the living God. And Jesus affirmed that beautiful fact before the crowd. With those words Jesus extended kinship to her. Not only did He restore Veronica to her community, but He welcomed her into divine community!

Just a few years later at Pentecost, we can assume that she received the life of God and became kin to divinity . . . a daughter of the most high God.

Jesus continued saying, "Your faith has made you well. Go in peace and be freed from your suffering." Veronica had suffered twelve long years. And now, *finally*, it was over. What doctors couldn't do, Jesus, the Great Physician, did. Where men failed, Jesus Christ succeeded.

No more a social outcast, the kingdom of God had broken into the muddy and muddled present of another desperate woman's life, exalting the mercy, tenderness, love, and compassion of the One who created all things.

Pressing into the Kingdom

In Matthew 11:12, Jesus said,

> From the days of John the Baptist until now the kingdom of heaven has suffered violence, and the violent take it by force.[8]

The parallel passage in Luke uses the phrase, "forcing their way into" the kingdom.

> The Law and the Prophets were proclaimed until John. Since that time, the good news of the kingdom of God is being preached, and everyone is forcing their way into it. (Luke 16:16)

Sometimes the Lord will put His children in a position where they become so desperate for Him that they will become motivated to "force their way into" His kingdom where there is "righteousness, peace and joy" (Rom. 14:17).

"Pressing into the kingdom" (as some translations put it) isn't just about salvation. It's about receiving the benefits of the kingdom, like deliverance, peace, and joy.

Veronica had no control over her condition. This lack of control pressed her into a profoundly desperate place. And when she heard about Jesus, she decided to violently "press into" the kingdom and "take it" by force. She had grown tired of the ostracism, the physical suffering, the abandonment, the pain, and the poverty, determined to receive her healing from the one Person she had yet to encounter: *Jesus of Nazareth.*

Perhaps when she heard the reports about Jesus healing others, she thought to herself, *If He healed them, then I'm determined to get near Him so that He can heal me too.*

Like the Canaanite woman who persisted to have the Lord heal her daughter—despite His ignoring, rebuffing, and even insulting her—Veronica persisted so she could receive from Jesus (Matt. 15:21–28). Here was a woman with a violent faith!

Sometimes the Lord wants us to wait and rest in Him. Other times, however, He wants us to press into His kingdom and receive what is rightfully ours in Christ.

Recall Jacob's encounter with the angel. Jacob wrestled with God and wouldn't let Him go until he received the blessing. On that night, Jacob pressed into what God wanted for him, exercising a violent faith.

In the same way, the two Hebrew spies, Joshua and Caleb, refused to be intimidated by the giants they saw in the promised land of Canaan. They rather walked "by

faith, not by sight" (2 Cor. 5:7 ESV). They took the kingdom by violence. They pressed in despite the odds set
against them.

Receiving What Is Yours

When we experience crisis in our lives, most of us alternate
between rock-solid determination and weakhearted second-
guessing. We listen to the voices of doubt that always cave
in to unbelief. And thereby we become double-minded,
deluding ourselves. When this happens, it becomes hard
to see clearly through the soothing haze of self-deception.

> Let perseverance finish its work so that you may be mature and
> complete, not lacking anything. If any of you lacks wisdom, you
> should ask God, who gives generously to all without finding fault,
> and it will be given to you. But when you ask, you must believe
> and not doubt, because the one who doubts is like a wave of the
> sea, blown and tossed by the wind. That person should not expect
> to receive anything from the Lord. Such a person is double-minded
> and unstable in all they do. (James 1:4–8)

Dear child of God, perhaps the Lord has allowed you to
be put into a desperate, hopeless situation beyond measure.
Maybe it's a case of intractable physical or emotional pain
that you've endured for years. Maybe it's an inexpressibly
painful relationship. Maybe it's a financial crisis.

Maybe it's something else tragic or traumatic. Like Veronica, you've tried to gain relief through every means
possible. You've prayed countless times. But there's been
no relief in sight, so you've given up.

Perhaps the Lord is wanting you to rise up . . . *today* . . . and force your way into His deliverance. Don't let Him go until He's blessed you[9] or until He says, "Leave it in my hands. My grace is sufficient for you."[10]

Perhaps He's calling you, right now, to be like Jacob, the two Hebrew spies, and Veronica . . . and determine that you will push your way through, to press in and to "touch" your Lord, receiving His goodness, mercy, and freedom.

Your desperation is designed to lead you to press into His kingdom by force.

The kingdom of God and all that's in it . . . righteousness, joy, and peace . . . belongs to you. It's your divine birthright.

> Do not be afraid, little flock, for your Father has been pleased to give you the kingdom. (Luke 12:32)

Never forget. When life crowds you with its pressures and problems, there is always room to stretch your hand toward the Lord Jesus and touch Him.

So remember Veronica's faith, risk, and determination, and go and do likewise.

5

Diary of the Woman Whom Jesus Loved

The perfume still scents my hands—hands that once dripped with my most precious possession, given joyfully to the One who became far more precious. But now the spikenard foretells death.

I am weeping as I dictate this. They have taken away my friend and Messiah in a mockery of justice. Judas led the hordes of club-holding, torch-wielding men and betrayed Jesus with a sickly sign of affection—a kiss, I am told.

They are jealous. I could see this bludgeoning rage on the streets of Bethany, could taste the envy as Jesus performed what the religious elite could not. Miracles. Forgiveness-granting. Sight to the blind. People restored to community. My brother, paradoxically alive—a living, breathing example of their paltry power over death. Only Jesus could command the dead to rise. Now He is imprisoned, destined to die.

And I am destined to weep the rest of my life because I have no such power over the grave. All I have is that deeper intuition granted by God that Jesus would be handed over, that His destiny would not end well. Which is why the perfume on my hands has become the scent of burial.

I am harried in the moment, sometimes. But when I pause to look back on life and identify its mountain moments, I see God's ways. They seem paradoxical at the time, confusing even, but in sweet retrospect, a pattern emerges—a divine tapestry, woven by providence and displayed as holy artifact as sure as the sun brightens a Passover day.

My story emerges in three entries, three acts, three stories. Three is a complete number, a triune semantic. Which is why I treasure each aha moment as spikenard. Because each interaction I share is not about abstract lessons from a prophet, priest, or king, but it is infused with relationship with my dear, dear Jesus—who is all those offices and more. He has praised my actions. He has challenged me. He has honored me. But no person has ever domesticated Him. I am simply grateful He sought and dignified me.

Story One. My brother Lazarus dared to invite a troupe of men into our home, a gaggle of beards, tunics, dirty feet, and appetites—all on the heels of our father Simon's healing by Jesus of Nazareth. The leprosy had whitened his arms, and the bandages soured day after day. Soon he would have faced alienation, something we all could not bear after the death of our mother, his betrothed.

You would think my father's healing would overshadow the entire day, but it was Jesus who outshone even freshly pinked skin.

So when Lazarus came yelling, and my father cried tears of astonishment, my sister Martha and I rushed to him. I worried his tears meant the authorities had ordered Father to vacate to the colony, but I soon realized his tears were of relief, not grief. We unwrapped his soaked bandages only to find virgin skin, clean and clear as a baby's after a bath. The four of us danced, shouted praise to the Almighty for such a beauty as healed skin.

"Who did this?" I asked.

"Jesus the Nazarene," Lazarus said.

"Jesus." His name tasted like honey on my tongue. I had heard of this holy man before. A prophet, some called Him. A rabble-rouser, the religious elite had proclaimed. A miracle worker, the children sang. I had wanted to meet Him, but this healing? Now I needed to thank Him.

Lazarus interrupted my mental meandering. "I have invited Him and His men for dinner. Thirteen in all."

Martha gasped. "Thirteen? Here? When?"

"Tonight." Lazarus said the word as if it meant no work for us, as if food would magically appear for these hungry men.

Martha grabbed my arm. "We must get food," she said.

My sister is blessed with hospitality; it pours from her like perspiration. She entangles herself with the needs of others, attends to people's hidden desires. Martha discerns their thirst before they even touch the roof of their mouths with parched tongue. That is my sister—so much like my mother. And I love her for her inclinations. What she perceives in tangible needs like this, I am cursed with knowing the matters of the heart. It is hard to measure helping a heart, so I often feel like Martha has greater satisfaction. She feeds; people are filled. I speak a word of encouragement, and I seldom know whether the words penetrate the heart.

We gathered figs, lamb, garlic, leeks, vegetables—and then we cooked. Men who wander the dusty streets are in wont of food, so she said, so we halved roots and butchered lamb, while Lazarus set the cook fires. In that moment, I felt such sweet peace, the three of us siblings working in tandem, as if we knew the Almighty smiled down upon us. The kitchen filled with the aroma of our laughter while my father prepared the central courtyard for guests. The pots clattered as we chattered about the guests who would arrive soon.

As the garlic sizzled, I heard His voice for the very first time.

I peeked around the opening that separated the kitchen from our main house. I saw many men in the throng, but One stood out. And where He stood, an angle of sunlight splashed one man's feet. "Jesus," I whispered.

Martha took a respite and watched. The men laughed, though they looked weary and disheveled. "I have heard He does not travel this earth alone. He always walks among

these twelve. Which is why I need your help." She stirred
another pot, lifting the broth to her mouth and blowing.

Strange that the aroma of savory food and the plea of my
sister had no power over me in that moment. I was not torn
between familial duty and Jesus. No. Jesus irresistibly drew
me the moment He sat and opened His mouth. I strained
to hear His words—sentences of life and heartache and
the kingdom of God flowed eloquently from His mouth.
I knew in that moment that whatever food we hastened
to prepare had no power to change a heart or heal a leper.
Victuals would only sustain a few hours, but this man's
words could fuel a well-lived life.

Honestly I do not know how it happened. I remember
stirring, idly keeping a semblance of conversation between
Martha and me. She made mention of needing some onions
and slipped away one hesitant moment. I heard Lazarus
and Jesus talking, but I could not make out exactly what
Jesus said. I wanted to have the conversation Lazarus easily
slipped into. I strained again to hear the words of Jesus, but
I could only make out snippets: *Kingdom of God. Least.
Blessed is. A certain man.* The words quickened something
within me, enticing my feet to do the impossible.

And in a hiccup, I found myself with Jesus. I took the
student's place, at the feet of the Rabbi. Had I been prop-
erly thinking, I would have let the male-scented situation
prevent me. I am not a bold woman. I know my place, particularly among a gathering of thirteen men—and Lazarus
and my father. But I paid them no mind at all. Only one
man's opinion seemed worth my pursuit—Jesus.

THE DAY I MET JESUS

I cannot tell you whether the men shouted or murmured or rebuked. I did not fear my father's rebuke, either. That Jesus welcomed me must have quieted them some. Not even Lazarus hushed my boldness. Perhaps because Jesus spoke to us all, and His words were unlike anything we had heard before. Words of grace. Of life. Of hope. Of peace.

His words bled me of the shame I had carried since a child, a monster I did not know clung to my shoulders my whole life. It had whispered, *You will never be enough. Your sins disqualify you from serving God. You do not possess the hospitality so valued in your sister. Or the conversational beauty of your brother. Or the holiness of your father. Or the sacrificial nature of your mother. You are the outsider, the thinker, the different one. You are fit for nothing but mulling over matters of the heart.* Until that moment at the Rabbi Jesus' feet, I had not realized the voice in my head was not the voice of God. Hearing His words awakened a small hope, a seed that perhaps might blossom into a vine, a flower, a grape, a cup of fine wine. Perhaps God had a plan for me—quirky, different me!

Jesus, in those sweet moments, revealed His life to me. His mission. His determination. His friendship. Were the others listening too? I do not know because the ray of light, with dust dancing like silver, circled us only. He reminded me that the kingdom He built exploded in contrasts, in unexpected, upside-down ways. The poor would be rich in love. The overlooked would learn to love as no other could. The weak would finally be strong. Those who came in last would find themselves first on the shores of heaven.

Those who lusted after greatness would, inevitably, inherit dishonor, while those who knew their place of lowliness would be lifted up by Jesus.

Oh, how He valued His people. Oh, how He loved us. I saw affection in His eyes. Not a lustful leer. But an all-consuming fire of *hesed* love. I basked in the joy of it, as the sun shifted from spotlighting us to make its journey up the rough walls of our courtyard. And when the shade cooled me, Martha's harried voice interrupted.

"Lord, does it not seem unfair to you that my sister just sits here while I do all the work? Tell her to come and help me!" Hands on hips, eyes narrowed, a huff in her voice—my sister disciplined me in front of the Teacher.

I shrunk inside myself, the place I had retreated so many times when I felt like I was an oddity of nature, a strange pilgrim on this earth whom no one truly understood, including myself. The familiar voices reminded me once again that I had shirked my responsibilities, failed to live up to expectations, and had no right to abandon my sister, violate every social code, and sit at this man's feet. I came to myself in that moment, realizing how shocking my behavior must have appeared—to Martha, to Lazarus, to my father, to those twelve hungry men. And most certainly, to Jesus.

I refused to respond to my sister. I would not defend myself.

I sat there patiently, prepared for a rebuke.

But He looked at me with those impossible, welcoming eyes. In that exchange I knew He wanted me to stay there. So I remained.

And waited afresh for the harsh shame.

"My dear Martha." Jesus pronounced her name with affection and a hint of kind humor. "Martha." Repeating her name dripped of His compassion. "You are worried and upset over all these details! There is only one thing worth being concerned about. Mary has discovered it, and it will not be taken away from her."

The room fell silent at His words. My face warmed. Was it embarrassment? Worry for how Martha may have felt? Fear?

I had not been rebuked, but praised! Dinner could wait in lieu of relationship. Conversation trumped cooking. Jesus actually welcomed my position at His feet, and He used me as a good example to the gathering around us.

As I dictate these words to scroll, I choose to ignore the rebukes touting my unworthiness. Instead I am turning over His words in my mind. *There is only one thing worth being concerned about. Mary has discovered it, and it will not be taken away from her.*

There is permanence with this Jesus, the One we affectionately call "Teacher." A lasting eternal hope. He breathes the words of life that obliterate shame and that feeling of smallness. My heart is deeply warmed, changed, and hopeful. And I know. *I know.* Jesus is the Messiah we have been longing for. I give my life to follow this Son of Man, Son of God, this Prince of Life.

But I have one glaring regret. I never thanked Him for healing my father.

Story Two. This day. How to summarize this day? Words seem a strange invention to frame death, life, and Jesus.

The dusk was a culmination of several days, of longing, of disappointment, of anguish. Lazarus caught a fever in the same manner our mother had. The heat settled into his chest, stood on it, letting in only fickle sips with each draw. Lazarus grabbed for air, held hostage by his lungs' faltering rhythm. His chest, hungry for sustenance, let the precious commodity exhale into the unknown. As he struggled, I held my breath. Willing that the pallor in his skin would become my rosiness. Yet, my pink belied his ashen face.

Martha fretted.

"Calm your anxious heart," I told her. I lifted a cool, wet cloth to Lazarus' hot forehead. "Jesus is the friend of Lazarus. We will send word, and He will come."

She held Lazarus' hand, looked into his frightened eyes. "Yes," she said. "Yes, let us do that right now."

Lazarus nodded, his eyes weak, his resolve to live slipping away moment by moment. So very tired, he looked.

Martha gave the following message to a young boy, "Lord, your dear friend, the one whom you love, is very sick." She instructed the courier to run as wind to Perea, where Jesus was staying. When the boy sprinted, Martha shouted after him, "Quickly, now." The hitch in her voice frightened me.

The hush in the house gave me pause. For a panicked moment, I wondered if Lazarus still brought in breath. Had we sent message to the Messiah too late? But my brother's chest rose and fell in the silence, and I continued my vigil next to him while Martha gave him a cool cup of water.

Father entered the room looking haggard. He had not kept watch as we had. Seeing another with the same fever that stole his wife from earth must have opened old wounds, and even older fears. "Why him?" he lamented. "Why not me? A child is not supposed to precede his father in death."

I shushed Father. Whispered, "Let us keep the faith. Do not despair just yet. We have summoned Jesus."

"Ah, yes. Jesus." Father's glinted eyes were a study in remembrance. He rubbed his supple skin, then smiled. "He will heal our Lazarus." Father left to get more water.

"Glory," Lazarus said, though the word was a whisper. "Glory."

"Jesus is coming. No need to fret," I told him. The words were more prayer than confidence. Because as the hours wore on and the sun slipped behind the horizon, Lazarus developed a rattle in his chest, and Jesus had not come. By now He would have received the message and stood here, by the side of His beloved friend. Our home was Jesus' respite, a place of life and laughter amid the barrage of needs that often pressed in around Him. Bethany had become His haven, and we, His grateful caretakers. When He unsandaled Himself after the threshold of our home, His tired eyes seemed to rest, and He would let out a long-held breath.

Surely He would welcome this diversion—particularly since it meant my brother's life teetered on the brink of the hereafter.

But as the night wore thin and stars pocked an impossibly black sky, my hope frayed and became threadbare. And when the boy came back without Jesus the next morning, I sunk into myself.

"Did you give Jesus the message?" I asked.

He nodded. "Yes."

"And?"

The boy shuffled his dirtied feet before me, eyes cast groundward.

"Did He say anything to you? Any word about His coming?"

"He said nothing to me, but He did turn to the men nearby and say, 'Lazarus's sickness will not end in death. No, it happened for the glory of God so that the Son of God will receive glory from this.'"

I let out a sigh, patted the boy on the head—a sign for him to leave, and found Martha and Father. "He will not die," I told them. We embraced. "The Teacher said the word." Out of earshot of our brother's labored breathing, we talked of Father's healing with a touch, and the rumors of other healings with a word from Jesus. Perhaps this was what Jesus meant. I knew His words wielded power, as I had sat beneath them, absorbed them, and experienced the transformation under His sweet tutelage. Yes, brother Lazarus would be well.

The day waned as dusk announced itself. And with the fall of night, Lazarus lost himself. He thrashed. Moaned. Called our names, though we remained resolute at his side. "Sing," he managed.

I sang the *shema* over him. "Listen, O Israel! The LORD is our God, the LORD alone. And you must love the LORD your God with all your heart, all your soul, and all your strength." Martha and Father joined the somber song, devoid of praise, pregnant with desperation. Lazarus, strengthless, mouthed the words with us, the four of us desperate for the God of Israel to rescue us from this peril.

No such rescue came.

At midnight the rattle in Lazarus' breath intensified. The panic in his eyes begged me to take this lonely journey with him. But I could not. I watched helplessly as he determined to breathe. In, then out. A hiccup. Another hiccup of the chest. Another sip of breath, a great letting out. It siphoned in through his parched lips, now a small O. His legs, once hale and muscular, now purpled to his knees. They were cold to the touch, and as I rubbed them, they grew colder still.

I looked at Martha, remembering the last moments of Mother's life, how we held this similar vigil before she left this earth. Mother, sickened for years, seemed eager to cross over to the embrace of heaven, but we grabbed at her, hoping to tear her away from the journey she already walked. We clawed, in a way, but she left our grasp willingly. And in that moment of death, Lazarus dutifully assumed his role as the strong one, the one we could depend on. Because after Mother died, grief and leprosy attacked Father. Our brother became a man then, and now he fought to keep breath in his lungs.

"You," he wheezed. "Will be." Another breath. "Safe."

Martha put her head on Lazarus' chest. "No, we will not. We need you. We love you. Do not leave!"

Father entered the room, eyes weary and red from crying. He put his arms around us both, while Martha cried.

Her emotions echoed mine, but I kept quiet, leaving Father's embrace to rub my brother's legs, wetting his lips with a dampened cloth once Martha pulled away. This is something I could do. Something tangible I could perform.

"The Master will come," I said plainly.

"He is not here right now," Martha said. "Do you not see how Lazarus is near the end?"

I shushed her. Motioned for her to leave the room with me. "Do not say those faithless words in his presence," I whispered.

"But death will overtake him within the hour. You know I have accompanied many on their final journeys. Death knocks at his door."

"Let us sing," I told her.

So we sang over Lazarus as God had been known to sing over Israel. With Father, we sang songs of deliverance. Of parting of the Red Sea. Of David's exploits. Of Jerusalem's captivity. Of Nehemiah's wall building. Of Isaiah's prophecies. This bolstered us both until Lazarus shot straight up in bed. For a moment, I felt Jesus must be near, healing our dear, dear brother. But Lazarus' eyes widened, a dance of fear and rapture in his eyes. He shouted "Glory!" then fell back onto his bed and exhaled life for the last time.

I wept.

Martha wept.

My father collapsed.

We held each other in grief, not wanting to believe we stood alone on this earth, no brother, no mother, just two women and an aging father without prospect for hope— our only insurance against starvation, an alabaster flax of spikenard that I had saved from Mother's sole possessions. We would need it sooner than later.

The wailers came, joining their professional grief with our genuine sorrow. We cried every tear, dried our bodies clear out, until we felt utterly, irrevocably spent.

That evening blurred as we prepared his body for burial, sweetening the eminent stench with herbs and spices. Lazarus grew stiffer and colder the longer we fussed with him, and no matter how many times I touched his hand, willing it back to life, it lay cold as a winter brick in mine.

And as we walked in procession toward the family tomb where Mother laid, and mourners sang their terribly sad songs, all I could think about was Jesus, how He could have prevented this tragedy, but for whatever reason, His faithfulness turned on me, until He embodied capriciousness. Not only was He not here to heal my brother in time, but He did not even show up at his funeral. And the words He said to the men around Him about the glory of God? All terrible lies.

Could Jesus always be trusted?

Were His words always true?

I struggled against these questions, though I did not give them voice.

The twin grief of Jesus not showing up to heal my brother or even bother to attend his funeral beat within me for four days. I had grieved everything, my whole life, my identity, and my faith wallowed. What kind of loving Son of God let His friend die, then rot in the grave? A very small part of me knew there must have been a reason, even though I could not grasp it.

Four days later while we still grieved, Martha pointed to the horizon as the dust from several men kicked up. "Jesus," she said. And before I could react to the declaration, she ran out of the house to meet Him. I remained inside with the circle of mourners, our friends. Martha returned, pulled me aside, and said, "The Teacher is here and wants to see you."

I went to Him.

Jesus remained outside the village at the same place Martha met Him. When the mourners saw me leave so hastily, they assumed I ventured to Lazarus' grave to weep. So they followed me there. When I arrived, I fell at Jesus' feet and said, "Lord, if only You had been here, my brother would not have died."

Jesus met my eyes. I saw sadness, compassion, and a snarl of anger there. He held my hand. "Where have you put him?" He asked the crowd.

One of the mourners said, "Lord, come and see."

At the hillside above Lazarus' and Mother's resting place, a crowd remained. So many loved my brother. And so many suffered grief in his absence. We walked toward the tomb, and as we did, I wondered if Jesus regretted not coming sooner.

I expected an answer to my question. Or maybe a soliloquy about the brevity of life. Or a sermon about grief. But Jesus said nothing.

The crowd noticed the Teacher. The murmuring and tears quieted in His presence. And then in the silence, I heard God cry. Not a gentle weeping, but a roar from the gut.

Jesus wept.

I wept.

The crowd wept.

We wet the dust with our tears.

One standing nearby said, "See how much He loved him!"

But His companion said, "This man healed a blind man. Could He not have kept Lazarus from dying?"

Jesus approached the tomb, a cave with a behemoth stone rolled across its entrance. "Roll the stone aside."

"Lord, he has been dead for four days," Martha said. "The smell will be terrible."

"Did I not tell you that you would see God's glory if you believe?" He said these words to me directly—the disciples, who by now had caught up with Him, and the peripheral crowd all heard them.

I wondered why the Teacher seemed to need closure with His friend. Did He want the stone rolled away so He could prove Lazarus' demise? Did He need to say His goodbyes? If that were so, why did He not come sooner?

But I remembered Lazarus' last word. *Glory*. And something that felt like hope, a flicker, tickled my heart.

Several men rolled the stone aside. The stench emanated, stinging my eyes. I covered my nose with a veil.

Jesus looked sunward, eyes squinting. "Father, thank You for hearing Me. You always hear Me, but I said it out loud for the sake of all these people standing here, so that they will believe You sent Me." He looked at Martha, then at me, a hint of a smile in His eyes.

"Lazarus, come out!" The words thundered, so stunning and terrible in their tenor that I simultaneously wanted to cover my ears yet welcome them still.

And then.

Then.

My brother Lazarus walked out of the tomb, hands and feet bound in graveclothes, his face wrapped in a headcloth. Muffled words in cadence came from the cloth suffocating his head. Time halted, but Lazarus kept repeating a word, yet with pitch. Our brother was singing!

Jesus looked at me, at Martha, at our father, then said to the others, "Unwrap him and let him go!"

I ran to him, then stood before him, while death's scent gripped my stomach. Decay and burial spices defied enlivened limbs and my brother's tenor voice—a beautiful paradox, this. I unwrapped his head, unleashing his worship, while I looked into dancing eyes.

"Life!" he said. "Life!"

"Yes" was all I could say. Because this word defined the moment. Once death, now life. From a graveclothes prison to the sun shining on supple skin.

As others shouted amazement around me, some shrieked in horror. I yelped, then embraced him. I cried.

He laughed.

I laughed.

I touched his face. "It is you?" I asked.

"I am no ghost," he said.

Father embraced him, tears between them. "My son," he repeated.

Martha grabbed Lazarus, kissed his very-much-alive cheek on the once-slack face we had embalmed with spices. His once cold hand now warmly embraced mine. The breathing that had labored and rasped now filled awakened lungs.

The word *miracle* thrummed through the crowd. Children lifted arms high to the heavens, and then danced around Jesus, smiles wide. Elders shook their heads as if they were seeing things, and the shaking would bring back the reality of Lazarus' death.

Except that Lazarus kept on living.

Women wept, but these were tears of astonishment.

A few religious leaders wore no such astonishment. Instead they scowled, and gathered in a circle, voices hushed, fingers pointing at Jesus, at Lazarus, at me, at Martha, at our father. The strange seriousness of their banter soured my stomach.

I looked away, told myself to memorize the beautiful parts of this moment. My brother, beautifully alive. He laughed. He danced. He swung children around on strong, strong limbs.

I caught his gaze as he set little Josiah down. He smiled at me. Then he shouted, "Glory!"

Glory, indeed.

Story Three. There are times you know in your gut that life will never be the same. A kind of sad omen takes over your heart and dread fills you full.

This should have been a joyful day, still aglow in the revelation that my brother walked this earth alive. News about his demise, then resurrection, bustled Bethany, then Judea. Folks kept stopping by, touching his face, clucking at the sky at the wonder of it all. But these very rejoicings accompanied a painful truth: in equal doses envy reigned. Mutterings of betrayal, greed, jealousy trickled in from the camp of the Pharisees. This Jesus had too much power, something they did not possess, other than their own small might over the masses. They who clamored after holy fame sought to take down the One who seemed to shun the limelight.

Yes, Jesus came to our home at our invitation in the midst of these stirrings. And I knew time would come when rumors turned to terrible reality. They would kill the One who resurrected my brother.

Once again we prepared a feast, Martha, Lazarus, Father, and myself. To honor the Messiah six days prior to the Passover Seder. To provide brief reprieve, a refreshing taste of life as He faced what would come. The men, hardened by world-weary fatigue, sat encircling Martha's feast, their conversation less animated than before. I remembered the first time we met Jesus, how I had bowed at His feet, welcoming good news from His lips. And now, we reprised our roles. Martha served with holy fervor (but with joy, not fretting), and I could not bring myself to join in the presentation of figs and olives and wine and fish.

Because I knew.

This would be the last time I saw my dear Jesus alive.

His was a life ended with purpose, to do the Father's will, even if that will meant death. And somehow His death would mean good news for those of us left behind, though my mind had difficulty understanding why that could possibly be so. How could death end in glory?

Lazarus made a joke, and roared backward in laughter. Ah, yes, glory.

But how could that be? Who would raise Jesus from the dead if Jesus were not there to do the miraculous raising?

Sorrow strangled me as I watched Jesus pat Lazarus on the back. They exchanged looks of knowing. My brother had no words to tell me, though I peppered him with questions about the hereafter, and what must it have been like being called from death to earth. But when those two looked at each other, I knew they held a secret—one Lazarus could not tell, and one Jesus would not reveal. The specter of death haunted us all.

And I knew it would hasten Jesus from this earth.

In that space, while men ate and murmured, while Martha puttered and prepped, I understood what needed to be done. The alabaster flask was never far from me—a gift my mother gave me as she lay dying. It represented my security, my future, nearly a year's worth of wages. Every time Lazarus coughed, I worried that he would taste death a second time, leaving Martha, Father, and me alone to fend for ourselves. That perfume would be our rescue.

The voice of God, slow and clear, rumbled inside me, reminding me of true security. *The Messiah needs this more than you.* Yes. He did.

I walked to the spikenard flask, opened it, and inhaled deeply. Such a medley of fragrance for such a tragically amazing man.

It had been my mother's, and she pressed it into my hands before her last breaths. "For provision," she said.

I crossed the room, sat at Jesus' feet, and began pouring out our livelihood in extravagant gulps. I watched the perfume flood over those worn feet. I took down my hair, using my tresses to spread the essence of nard through His toes, the tops and bottoms of His feet, up to His ankles. Then I poured the last portion on His head, while the fragrance dripped down His beard and teardropped onto his tunic. The room pulsed with scent, and in that moment I knew I had anointed my King for burial.

"That perfume was worth a year's wages." Judas' voice dripped shame and sarcasm in equal doses. "It should have been sold and the money given to the poor."

To my shame, the other disciples of Jesus chimed in, agreeing with Judas. I wanted to retreat to the kitchen this time, to rid myself of Judas' very true statement. Perhaps I had been wasteful?

Jesus put His hand on my arm, briefly—a sign to stay where I sat.

"Leave her alone," He said. "She did this in preparation for My burial." The men around the table gasped. Jesus nodded, and as He did, I could see the truth in His words. He would die. I knew before He said it, but His words confirmed my grief. "You will always have the poor among you, but you will not always have Me." His words sombered us all, cast a pallor of death over our group. Jesus, the resurrector, would die. And soon. The perfume which had scented the room with life now hinted at burial. He looked right at me, right through me, actually, and cleared His throat. "I tell you the truth, wherever the Good News is preached throughout the world, this woman's deed will be remembered and discussed."

I shook my head as His words of praise echoed through my soul. Why would such a man say these things? To me? My act seemed small in comparison to the reward He offered.

I end this day with spikenard hands, a remembrance of Jesus, His words, *You will not always have Me*, lumbering through me. Oh, that such a perfume would remind Him of our love at His darkest hour. I cherished His words about Good News and my simple act of love, hoping they would bring comfort in the dark days ahead.

I am living in the midst of these darkened days while Jesus languishes as a prisoner. I weep into my hands, willing the remaining scent to linger there forever in tribute. But I know this life. I know its inevitabilities. The best of people die before their time—just as my Lazarus did. And eventually my perfume-baptized hands will smell of death and grief.

And yet, oddly, a trace of hope quickens my heart. This kingdom Jesus spoke of to us in our Bethany home rumbles inside me. And although I fear the immediate future, I believe that the Father has plans I am unaware of. So I finish this entry as a broken woman with a flask of hope. King David's words sing through me though my eyes leak tears. "Yet I am confident I will see the LORD's goodness while I am here in the land of the living."[1]

That is my hope.

THE SACRED TEXT

Now it happened as they went that He entered a certain village; and a certain woman named Martha welcomed Him into her house. And she had a sister called Mary, who also sat at Jesus' feet and heard His word. But Martha was distracted with much serving, and she approached Him and said, "Lord, do You not care that my sister has left me to serve alone? Therefore tell her to help me." And Jesus answered and said to her, "Martha, Martha, you are worried and troubled about many things. But one thing is needed, and Mary has chosen that good part, which will not be taken away from her."

—Luke 10:38–42 NKJV

Now a man named Lazarus was sick. He was from Bethany, the village of Mary and her sister Martha. (This Mary, whose brother Lazarus now lay sick, was the same one who poured perfume on the Lord and wiped his feet with her hair.) So the sisters sent word to Jesus, "Lord, the one you love is sick."

When he heard this, Jesus said, "This sickness will not end in death. No, it is for God's glory so that God's Son may be glorified through it." Now Jesus loved Martha and her sister and Lazarus. So when he heard that Lazarus was sick, he stayed where he was two more days, and then he said to his disciples, "Let us go back to Judea." . . .

On his arrival, Jesus found that Lazarus had already been in the tomb for four days. Now Bethany was less than two miles from Jerusalem, and many Jews had come to Martha and Mary to comfort them in the loss of their brother. When Martha heard that Jesus was coming, she went out to meet him, but Mary stayed at home.

"Lord," Martha said to Jesus, "if you had been here, my brother would not have died. But I know that even now God will give you whatever you ask."

Jesus said to her, "Your brother will rise again."

Martha answered, "I know he will rise again in the resurrection at the last day."

Jesus said to her, "I am the resurrection and the life. The one who believes in me will live, even though they die; and whoever lives by believing in me will never die. Do you believe this?"

"Yes, Lord," she replied, "I believe that you are the Messiah, the Son of God, who is to come into the world."

After she had said this, she went back and called her sister Mary aside. "The Teacher is here," she said, "and is asking for you." When Mary heard this, she got up quickly and went to him. Now Jesus had not yet entered the village, but was still at the place where Martha had met him. When the Jews who had been with Mary in the house, comforting her, noticed how quickly she got up and went out, they followed her, supposing she was going to the tomb to mourn there.

When Mary reached the place where Jesus was and saw him, she fell at his feet and said, "Lord, if you had been here, my brother would not have died."

When Jesus saw her weeping, and the Jews who had come along with her also weeping, he was deeply moved in spirit and troubled. "Where have you laid him?" he asked.

"Come and see, Lord," they replied.

Jesus wept.

Then the Jews said, "See how he loved him!"

But some of them said, "Could not he who opened the eyes of the blind man have kept this man from dying?"

Jesus, once more deeply moved, came to the tomb. It was a cave with a stone laid across the entrance. "Take away the stone," he said.

"But, Lord," said Martha, the sister of the dead man, "by this time there is a bad odor, for he has been there four days."

Then Jesus said, "Did I not tell you that if you believe, you will see the glory of God?"

So they took away the stone. Then Jesus looked up and said, "Father, I thank you that you have heard me. I knew that you always hear me, but I said this for the benefit of the people standing here, that they may believe that you sent me."

When he had said this, Jesus called in a loud voice, "Lazarus, come out!" The dead man came out, his hands and feet wrapped with strips of linen, and a cloth around his face.

Jesus said to them, "Take off the grave clothes and let him go."

—John 11:1–7, 17–44

Six days before the Passover Jesus came to Bethany, where Lazarus lived (the man whom Jesus raised from the dead). There at Bethany they prepared dinner for him at the home of Simon the leper. Martha was serving, and Lazarus was one of those eating with him.

Then Mary took an alabaster jar of expensive ointment (a pound of pure nard) and came up to him as he reclined at the table. She broke the jar and poured the ointment over his head. She anointed his feet and wiped his feet with her hair. The house soon was filled with the aroma of the ointment.

When his disciples saw what she did, some became indignant and said to themselves, "Why is this ointment being wasted? This could have been sold for a considerable amount of money." So they began to rebuke her. Judas Iscariot (who would later betray him) said, "Why wasn't this ointment sold for a year's wages, and the money given to the poor?" He didn't say this because he was at all concerned about the poor, but because he was a thief and had charge of the money pouch and kept stealing what was put into it.

Jesus was aware of all this and said to them, "Leave her alone. Why are you bothering the woman? She has done a good thing for me. She has saved this ointment for the day of my burial. You always have the poor with you and can help them whenever you want, but you won't always have me. She has done what she could. In pouring out this oint-ment she has anointed my body for burial. I tell you the truth, wherever in the world this good news is proclaimed, what this woman has done will also be recounted in memory of her."

Many of the Jews who knew he was there came not only because of Jesus but because they wanted to see Lazarus, whom Jesus had raised from the dead. That is why the chief priests discussed how they might also kill Lazarus. On account of him a large number of Jews were leaving them and believing in Jesus.[2]

—See Matthew 26:6–13; Mark 14:3–9; and John 12:1–11

WALKING IT OUT

Mary of Bethany is one of our heroes. To our minds, she is among the most admirable people in all the Gospels. Even outshining the twelve apostles.

The typical caricatures we find in many commentaries about Mary are simply false. The idea that she was a "contemplative" who didn't care about service, that she was a selfish worshiper, that she was too heavenly minded to be any earthly good are staunchly contradicted by the Gospels.

Keep these five things in mind when you think about Mary of Bethany:

1. Mary was bitterly criticized on two separate occasions. Once by her sister and another time by the Twelve. And on both occasions, Jesus defended and commended her.

2. In three separate accounts where Mary is mentioned in the Gospels, she is found in the same exact posture: *Sitting at Jesus' feet*.[3]

3. Jesus said that wherever the gospel would be preached from the first century onward, the story of what Mary did for Him during His last days on earth would be proclaimed, remembered, and honored. Wow!

4. While Jesus loved everyone, the Gospels specifically say that He loved Mary, Martha, and Lazarus (John 11:5). His love for Mary and her siblings was an uncommon, though not improper, affection.

5. Mary lived in Jesus' favorite place on earth . . . *Bethany*. He was rejected everywhere else. It was in Bethany that the Son of God deliberately spent the last week of His earthly life.[4]

For all of these reasons, we have a lot to learn from this amazing woman and her encounters with her remarkable Savior.

The Heart of Mary

On the day she first met Jesus, Mary helped her sister Martha prepare a meal for Jesus and His disciples. Martha's initial complaint reveals this. Martha accused Mary of leaving her. That suggests that she did help Martha before she slipped into the public room to hear Jesus teach.

In the first century, they divided houses into the male space and the female space. The kitchen (the courtyard) became the sphere of the women. The public room (the living area) constituted the sphere of the men. And neither sex was supposed to cross over either barrier.

So Mary's act of moving into the public room with the men was not merely socially awkward—it bordered on high offense.

But Mary did something else scandalous. She sat at Jesus' feet. Sitting at someone's feet was the posture of a disciple. And in the first century, teachers like Jesus only had male disciples.

So Mary's act of sitting in the men's area (the public room) and sitting in the posture of a disciple should curry our admiration.

Here is a woman who was hungrier to learn from Jesus than she was to obey customs or traditions. And she refused to let propriety stop her from sitting at the Master's feet and becoming one of His disciples.

What is more, Mary seemed to instinctively know that Jesus would praise both of these acts, even though they represented cultural taboos.

She guessed right. He elevated both.

When Martha chided her sister for acting like a man, leaving her to work in the kitchen, Jesus defended Mary.

The fact that Mary didn't defend herself tells us something vitally important about her. It shows us that she valued humility, understood the power of brokenness, and willingly submitted to the hand of God.

The story makes clear that Martha's act of serving sprung from good motivation, though misguided. Jesus revealed this when He contrasted the "many things" (that Martha worried about) with the "one thing" (that Mary gave herself to).

The "one thing" is actually a person—Jesus Himself. And the "better thing" is to sit at His feet, to become His disciple.

But what does being a disciple mean exactly?

The Gospels make clear that a disciple is someone who

1. Embraces humility, brokenness, and the willingness to die to self (Luke 9:23–24).
2. Treats others the way they want to be treated in the same situation (Matt. 7:12).
3. Submits to and learns from the Master at any cost (Luke 14:25–34).

In all these ways, Mary modeled the life of a disciple.

"One thing is needful," the Lord said about Mary. "And I won't take it away from her." What high praise coming from the lips of Deity. Oh to be like Mary in our day.

Two Ways of Serving

In our observation and experience, every Mary used to be a Martha at one time.

What do we mean?

Simply this. The Marthas of the Christian world are those who have been taught that the main thing that God desires of us is service. He wants us to do many things for Him. He wants us to be missional, to make converts, and then to turn those converts into disciples. He has a big to-do list.

The Marthas of this world are very busy doing good things. But eventually, they burn out or bail out. Why? Because they operate in their own power. And their priorities become crooked.

They are trying to do something for God, yet haven't learned the secret of letting God live in and through them where *He* is doing the work.

> Don't you believe that I am in the Father and the Father is in me?
> The words I speak are not my own, but my Father who lives in
> me does his work through me. (John 14:10 NLT)

Countless Christians live each day out of guilt, condemnation, religious duty, and obligation, trying to win brownie points with God by doing, doing, and more doing. They feel happy when they check off a spiritual task, but they also embrace condemnation when they haven't created enough checks in a day. To them, the Christian life is a treadmill where you trip and fall, or you run-run-run and never arrive. In light of this, some burn out, growing tired of serving altogether. So they create an aversion to any kind of Christian service. Others bail out. They stop following the Lord all together because they feel that their service for God has gained them nothing. Because their eyes stay fixed on their own work for the Lord (as Martha's were), they judge their fellow disciples who haven't done as much as them, yet who seemingly enjoy God's blessing on their lives.

So they conclude: What's the use? Why am I doing all of this for God when He's blessing these others—who aren't doing a fraction of what I do—more than He's blessing me?

Don't make the mistake of thinking that Mary didn't serve the Lord. She certainly did. But her service was rooted in something higher than duty or obligation. And it wasn't motivated by fear, outward applause, condemnation, or guilt. The "one thing" motivated Mary. Paul talked about this "one thing" better than we can. He wrote,

> But whatever were gains to me I now consider loss for the sake of Christ. What is more, I consider everything a loss because of the surpassing worth of knowing Christ Jesus my Lord, for whose sake I have lost all things. I consider them garbage, that I may gain Christ. . . . I want to know Christ—yes, to know the power of his resurrection and participation in his sufferings. . . . Brothers and sisters, I do not consider myself yet to have taken hold of it. But one thing I do: Forgetting what is behind and straining toward what is ahead. (Phil. 3:7–10, 13)

In light of this, look at Mary again and take your cue from her. Learn what she understood—that being a disciple isn't about serving or keeping a spiritual to-do list. It's first and foremost about opening your heart and listening to Jesus, spending time with Him. It's about being teachable, sitting at His feet. It's about humility, acknowledging that He knows best how we should live our lives. It's about loving Him, forsaking even important tasks for the sake of revering Him alone.

Jesus Himself followed the example of Mary, for after she anointed His feet (John 12), He washed the feet of His disciples (John 13). Mary knew what servanthood was, and Jesus honored her example.

And out of those values will flow everything else. Including service and mission.

Response to Tragedy

Mary only speaks once in the Gospels. But her actions utter volumes.

In John 11, we have the only recorded words from Mary.

When Mary heard that Jesus had just entered the village of Bethany, she dropped everything and ran out to greet Him. When Mary caught up with Jesus outside the village, the Lord was deeply troubled. The Greek word translated "troubled" or "agitated" in John 11:33 actually means indignation. He also shed tears.

Why was He indignant? Why did He weep?

The Lord's tears revealed His sensitivity to human pain and suffering. Jesus was deeply moved by the sorrow that His good friends, Mary and Martha, felt by losing their brother.

> For we have not an high priest which cannot be touched with the feeling of our infirmities; but was in all points tempted like as we are, yet without sin. (Heb. 4:15 KJV)

As I (Frank) put it in *God's Favorite Place on Earth*,

> In our suffering, we want an explanation. But Jesus wants to give us a revelation . . . of Himself. . . .
>
> Every crisis in our lives is an opportunity to broaden, deepen, and heighten our revelation of Christ.
>
> In Bethany, we discover a God who is willing to wait until it's too late.[5]

Every person who has followed the Lord for a while can testify to this shocking truth: God has a disturbing habit of leaving the scene when we most need Him. When things get really bad, He often seems to disappear.

This happens throughout Scripture, one of the most blaring being during Hezekiah's reign. Read what happened to the king at his moment of need: "However, when ambassadors arrived from Babylon to ask about the remarkable events that had taken place in the land, God withdrew from Hezekiah in order to test him and to see what was really in his heart" (2 Chron. 32:31 NLT). Sometimes God tests our faith, not to abandon us, but to grow us closer to Him in the long run.

When her brother died and Jesus didn't show up to heal him, His surprising absence tested Mary's newfound faith. Especially in light of the fact that He seemingly promised that Lazarus would not die.

> Jesus said, "This sickness will not end in death. No, it is for God's glory so that God's Son may be glorified through it." (John 11:4)

To add to her pain, Jesus didn't show up for the funeral. In the first century, if close friends missed the funeral of their loved ones, it constituted a great embarrassment to the grieving family—an offense not easily forgiven.

In this instance, Matthew 11:6 is instructive. There Jesus said, "Blessed is the one who is not offended by me."[6]

While Mary struggled with giving in to offense, she overcame her struggle. Consider Mary's words: "Lord, if You only had been here, my brother would not have died."

These words are familiar to all of us. "Lord, if You only had . . . then I wouldn't be in this position."

But Mary's faith does not disintegrate. In fact, her tears of genuine pain and disappointment provoke Jesus to weep.

He then said, "Show me where he is." And the Lord turns a four-day-old death into a life-giving resurrection.

Jesus raises Lazarus from the dead.

In this story, we again find a Lord full of surprises. This should serve as a gentle warning: If Jesus isn't surprising us, then we may have stopped growing spiritually.

Mary shows us how to believe in the face of doubt, distress, and disillusionment. She shows us how to weep in a way that evokes the empathetic tears of God. She shows us how to cease being offended at a God who confounds us.

An Uncommon Banquet

Near the end of the Lord's life on earth, Mary and Martha held a banquet to honor Jesus and celebrate Lazarus' resurrection.

Martha served, but she was no longer worried or troubled like she was when she first met Jesus. Something had shifted in her heart. That's what staying around Jesus will do. It changes us from the inside out.

For the third time in the Gospel of John, Mary sits at the feet of Jesus.

Mary knew the Lord's feet very well.

Matthew and Mark say that she anointed His head. John says she anointed His feet. She did both.

Luke writes about an earlier occasion when in the house of Simon (a Pharisee), a sinful woman washed the Lord's feet and dried them with her hair before anointing Him (Luke 7:38).

It's likely that Mary knew about that incident and was inspired by it. If so, Mary was disclaiming any merit and identifying herself with a great sinner. Point: All true worshipers feel the same when they are at the feet of Christ. We are nothing, and He is everything.[7]

Mary poured the costly perfume she owned upon Jesus' head (the way kings were anointed) and afterward, His feet.

She anointed Him as one would prepare a corpse for burial. Mary seemed to instinctively know that her king would soon die.

The Value of Christ

The perfume she had was worth three hundred denarii—a full year's wage.

Scholars speculate that Mary probably received the perfume as a family heirloom. So it represented her future savings, her security.

Recall what Paul said in Philippians 3:8:

> I consider everything a loss because of the surpassing worth of
> knowing Christ Jesus my Lord, for whose sake I have lost all things.
> I consider them garbage, that I may gain Christ.

John makes special mention that she broke the alabaster flask scenting the house with the sweet aroma of the perfume. The flask reminds us of the earthly treasure that holds the life of Christ. It is only when we become broken vessels in God's hands that He can multiply His life in us and feed others. It's only when the alabaster flask of our self-life is broken that the scent of Jesus can be detected and enjoyed by those we touch.

Judas' bitter critique of her action is found here: "Why are you being so wasteful? You could have sold this perfume and given the money to the poor."

To their discredit, the other disciples chimed in with Judas.

Matthew's arrangement of the narratives is especially noteworthy. How much is Jesus worth? He was worth lavishing everything on Him, as "the woman" (Mary of Bethany) demonstrated. Then the disciples criticized her act—that was too much. He wasn't worth it.

Finally, Judas went and sold Jesus for thirty pieces of silver—the price of a slave in the law of Moses.

Three contrasting estimates of the worth of Christ with Mary being the role model for us.

Indeed, none of the other disciples understood the true worth of Jesus, and they were yet to grasp His inevitable fate. But Mary did. And her actions proved it.

For the second time in the Gospel of John, Mary is misunderstood and rebuked. Still she never defended herself. She exemplified Jesus as He stood before His accusers, silent. She embodied the proverb, "Even fools are thought wise when they keep silent; with their mouths shut, they seem intelligent" (Prov. 17:28 NLT). And she received the blessing of letting another praise her. "Let someone else praise you, not your own mouth—a stranger, not your own lips" (Prov. 27:2 NLT).

Those who defend themselves will not have the Lord to defend them. They will not hear His life-affirming words.

Those who defend themselves reveal their unbrokenness and pride. In this state, all they can hear is the sound of their own voice.

Mary was silent, and Jesus defended her again. "Why are you bothering this woman? She has done a beautiful thing to Me," He says.

To waste something is to give more than is required. In effect, Judas says, "The Lord isn't worth the price of this perfume."

If you will walk in the steps of Mary and give what's most precious to Jesus, people—even fellow Christians—will say you're wasting your life.

And if you don't respond in self-defense, Jesus will defend you. His response to such is always, "Let her alone . . . Let him alone. They have done a beautiful thing for Me." Your job is not to micromanage your reputation. It's to live for His. God sees everything and is best equipped to defend you.

Even now as you read these words, ask yourself if there is something in your life—or within your reach—that you can "waste" upon Jesus.

Learn to be like Mary and waste that which is most precious to you on Jesus. For only by wasting ourselves on Christ do we live life to its highest and fullest purpose. And in light of that, remember that nothing "wasted" for His kingdom is ever, truly wasted.

Every sacrifice we make, every quiet, unseen act of love, is chronicled by our Savior for that day when our deeds will be made known in the next life. You may struggle today wondering if all your quiet serving means anything in this splashy flashy world. You may not be heralded. You may be overlooked. There are days when you feel unnoticed, an outcast to the trendy crowd. Take courage in your service. God sees you. He does. He is the great Noticer. So waste your heart for His sake.

Anything less is the real waste.

6

One More Thing

Our goal in this book is to bring the Gospels to life in your eyes. We trust, therefore, that you will never see these five women the same again. More importantly, we hope you will find in Jesus, your Lord, a God who is greater, more interesting, and more compelling than ever before—so blessedly alive you can touch Him.

To sum up, who were these five women, exactly?

An adulteress caught in the act.

A prostitute who dared to love Jesus in the house of a Pharisee.

A multiple divorcée currently living in sin.

A patient with a flow of blood, thus rendering her defiled and isolated.

A friend, one of Jesus' greatest and most-loved disciples. This particular woman, Mary of Bethany, wasn't asked to "sell all" and "follow" Jesus. Instead, she and her family made a home for Christ in their little village when every other place had rejected Him.

All of these women reveal different aspects of the greatness of Jesus, and His relentless love for them. But more, they remind us of the words of John: "We love Him because He first loved us" (1 John 4:19 NKJV).

Each woman loved Jesus because He first loved them. And if He loved those broken women, you can be assured of His love for you too.

We do well to remember that during the time of Jesus, women had very few rights, certainly less than what most Western women experience now. Even so, a great multitude of women in the Majority World today find themselves in marginalized situations, prohibited from lending their voice to vote, demoted to second- and third-class citizenship, viewed as property instead of humanity.

Many of them are enslaved, exploited, and poverty-stricken, and cannot escape abusive relationships. Recent prominent books like *Half the Sky* by Nicholas D. Kristof and Sheryl WuDunn uncover the disparity and desperation countless women face today. Right now, in this very moment, many women face these same discriminations even in the body of Christ.[1]

Jesus and Women

As we look at Jesus and how He interacted with women, we see Him dignifying, validating, and championing them—all in contrast to a misogynist culture.

In addition, women played a prominent role in Jesus' earthly ministry. As John Bunyan put it, "They were women that wept when he was going to the cross, and women that followed him from the cross, and that sat by his sepulcher when he was buried. They were women that was [sic] first with him at his resurrection morn, and women that brought tidings first to his disciples that he was risen from the dead."[2]

In an ancient world, where many disregarded the testimony of women, Jesus' high regard for them bordered on the scandalous. The fact that all these accounts are included in the Canon of Scripture actually verify the resurrection accounts of Christ. Remember, God saw fit that the first eyes to behold the risen Jesus were those of a woman—all during an era where a woman's testimony had no credibility in a court of law.

Women, therefore, were the first evangelists.

The only way a man can discover how to treat a woman is by looking at how Jesus interacted with them. Your Lord was the defender of women.

He stepped in to save a broken, scandalized woman from the murderous plot of a group of self-righteous men. He lifted the weight of her shame, writing a new destiny for her in the dirt.

He saw value in an "unclean" Samaritan woman who was disregarded, despised, and viewed as damaged goods.

He honored a prostitute in the house of a Pharisee.

He healed a pariah woman whose flow of blood excommunicated her.

He exalted a woman who anointed Him for burial by commissioning her story to be rehearsed wherever the gospel message was heard.

He never talked down to a woman, but made them heroes in His parables.

And that for which Jesus came to die was a woman . . . *His* woman, the very bride of Christ.

Put simply, your Lord is in the business of loving, honoring, and defending women.[3] And God chose the womb of a woman to enter this world.

One Thing to Remember

Paul reminded us, "There is no longer Jew or Gentile, slave or free, male and female. For you are all one in Christ Jesus" (Gal. 3:28 NLT). When Jesus lived, died, and was resurrected, He removed the curse of sin, of separation, of enmity. At the foot of the Christ's cross, we are all one. We are all beloved children of God, not one gender or nationality or station greater than the other.

This is good news for everyone—Jew or Gentile, slave or free, male or female. God fulfilled what the Psalmist wrote so long ago: "He bowed the heavens and came down; thick darkness was under his feet" (Ps. 18:9 ESV). He who was Light dared to stoop to this dark earth, full of wars and slavery and pain to muddy His life with ours. He walked in our pain so we could know once and for all that God understands our plight.

As the writer of Hebrews put it, "For we do not have a

high priest who is unable to sympathize with our weaknesses, but one who in every respect has been tempted as we are, yet without sin. Let us then with confidence draw near to the throne of grace, that we may receive mercy and find grace to help in time of need" (Heb. 4:15–16 ESV).

In light of all of these startling truths, may you, dear Christian, encounter the same glorious Christ that these women encountered, and lift your voice to tell the world about that day—the day that you too encountered Jesus.

Whether you are a woman or a man, Jesus Christ is the greatest lover in the universe. And He wishes to love, defend, honor, and cherish you. This is the one thing you must always remember. The Christ that you've seen in this book is the same Christ that lives inside of all who have repented and believed upon His glorious name.

With that in mind, may you go in peace.

Talking It Over

We wrote these questions to help you interact with the biblical narrative, either by yourself or in a group setting.

Chapter 1

1. What part of this narrative (the woman caught in adultery) moved you the most and why?
2. Has someone you trusted ever set you up to be exposed like this woman was? Explain.
3. Jesus often frustrated people because He didn't play their games. He didn't answer the Pharisees' questions, but instead wrote in the dirt. Has Jesus ever confounded or surprised you by the way He responded? Explain.
4. While it's fine to judge actions, it's always wrong to impute motives to a person's heart. Only God has that ability and right. Describe a time when someone

    wrongly judged your intentions. Explain how it made you feel and what it did to the relationship.

5. Have you ever been in a situation where you felt that your life was over—physically, financially, or emotionally—and Jesus rescued you? Explain.

6. Why do you think the older people left the circle of stone-throwers first? What does this tell us about the influence of age on one's understanding of sin?

7. What have you learned afresh about Jesus through this encounter?

Chapter 2

1. What part of this narrative (the prostitute who loved Jesus) moved you the most and why?

2. What practical implications does the fact that Jesus was/is a friend of sinners have on your life right now?

3. What does extravagant, abandoned worship look like in your life today?

4. How does the example of the prostitute who "loved much" help you to love Christ without shame?

5. In contrasting the scribes and Pharisees with this woman, what are the qualities of a person's character that Jesus rebukes?

6. How does hearing this prostitute's story help you empathize with women trapped in the sex industry?

7. Have you ever been a Pharisee to someone else, and have you ever had a Christian act like a Pharisee toward you? Explain.

Chapter 3

1. What part of this narrative (Photine, the Samaritan woman) moved you the most and why?

2. How would many evangelical Christians regard Photine today and why?

3. Jesus crossed cultural barriers to talk to Photine—ethnically and gender-wise. Why do you think He did that?

4. Jesus taught Photine one of the highest things about worship that He ever taught anyone. Given the kind of checkered past that Photine had, what does this tell you about your Lord?

5. The next time you meet someone who has a past like Photine's (maybe not as severe or perhaps worse), how will you view them differently after reading this book?

6. In what ways does Photine's story show how Jesus dignified and empowered women?

7. Jesus told Photine about her past, but He did so in a way that set her free instead of shaming and condemning her. How might this be helpful as you parent your children, love your spouse, treat your employees, or be a friend to those you love?

Chapter 4

1. What part of this narrative (Veronica, the woman with the flow of blood) moved you the most and why?

2. After reading the "Walking It Out" section, what in Veronica's story was new to you?

3. How has this chapter inspired you to "press into" the kingdom and receive what is yours like Veronica did? Be specific.

4. If you were able to interview Veronica, what questions would you ask her that aren't revealed in the Gospels?

5. What does Veronica's story teach us about faith?

6. Why do you think Jesus kept asking who touched Him?

7. Explain how Caleb and Joshua, Jacob (when wrestling with the angel), and the Canaanite woman (with a sick daughter) were of the same spirit as Veronica.

Chapter 5

1. What part of this narrative (Mary of Bethany) moved you the most and why?

2. In what ways are you like Martha, and in what ways are you like Mary?

3. What are some ways that you can sit at Jesus' feet and hear His word today?

4. What does Mary's reaction to criticism teach us about not defending ourselves when under unjust attack or even constructive criticism?

5. Have you ever encountered the side of God where He didn't meet your expectations or seem to fulfill His promises? Explain.

6. Why do you think the disciples chimed in with Judas' harsh criticism of Mary and what can we learn from this?

7. Name three lessons you can take away from Mary of Bethany's example.

Chapter 6

1. Which of the five women featured in this book do you relate to the most and why?

2. Which one of the five narratives moved you the most and why?

3. Make a list of why each of the five women was an outcast and/or was criticized. What does this teach you about how Jesus views those things that people rejected them for?

4. If Jesus were physically on the earth today and lived in *your* city, what kind of people do you think He would hang out with and where would He spend much of His time? Be specific.

5. In what ways has this book caused you to view people's failures, mistakes, and sins differently?

6. In what ways has this book caused you to view your failures, mistakes, and sins differently?

7. In what ways has this book caused you to see Jesus in a new light?

The Veronica Project

We want to thank you so much for reading our book!

What a deep honor to co-write it. The process was difficult at times, but we felt the Lord's nearness and enablement as we crafted each chapter. So we are thankful to the Lord for the opportunity to serve Him and the body of Christ in this way.

We are also grateful to the Baker team for deciding to publish it and our agents Greg Daniel and Esther Fedorkevich for turning the idea into the printed product.

In addition, we're deeply thankful to Craig Keener for being our historical advisor. Craig ensured that every chapter was true to first-century history and the New Testament.

In honor of Veronica, the name the ancient Christians gave to the woman with the issue of blood, as well as all the other women we've featured in this book, we want to tell you about *The Veronica Project*.

Very often, our readers have expressed appreciation for how our books have impacted their lives. And they ask what they can do to let others know about the books so others can be blessed.

That's where *The Veronica Project* comes in. If you have been touched by the message of this book, we want to make it easy for you share it with your friends and family. *The Veronica Project* makes this incredibly simple.

Just go to **TheDayIMetJesus.com** and you will find the following:

- A "Taste Test" of the book to share with others so they can sample it.
- Free audios from live conferences.
- An audio course that delves deeper into the content of the book.
- A forum where you can ask us questions or make comments about the book.
- Discounts on bulk copies of the book to give as gifts to your friends and family.
- Testimonies of those who have been touched by the book (along with simple instructions on how you can add your own testimony, if you like).
- Ready-made tweets about the book to share on your Twitter feed and Facebook page.
- Inspirational "pins" and "images" to share on your Pinterest and Facebook pages.
- Banners to upload to your blog or website.

And much more.

Thank you again!

Warmly in Christ,
Frank & Mary
TheDayIMetJesus.com

Notes

Why We Wrote This Book

1. It is our intention to stay as close to the biblical narrative as possible. We have consulted other outside scholarly works to flesh out the stories—the setting, culture, and way of life. These details aren't meant to take away from the raw honesty of the stories but rather to enhance them and help you, as the reader, to identify even more closely with them. Our stories are, therefore, biblical narrative.

Introducing Five Amazing Encounters

1. Some scholars believe this based on John 19:25 and Luke 24:18.
2. I (Frank) give credit to N. T. Wright for this insight.
3. See Genesis 3:7.

Chapter 1: Diary of a Woman Caught in Adultery

1. ESV.
2. Jesus had followers who were devout, observant Jews as well as followers who were not as devout and loved His teachings on grace and mercy.
3. Much of Jesus' teaching in the Sermon on the Mount (Matt. 5–7) is the dislodging of double standards that were taken for granted in Jewish culture. While Pharisaic ethics agreed much with Jesus'

teaching on the Mount, their fixation on legal details obscured this. Thus it's not enough to agree with Jesus' ethics. We need our hearts transformed, the very thing the Lord's critics needed but didn't possess.

4. Think of Judah in Genesis 38:24–26. Both he and Tamar sinned, but Judah condemned only Tamar. Judah was a sinner and a hypocrite.

5. Philip Yancey, *What's So Amazing About Grace?* (Grand Rapids: Zondervan, 2008).

Chapter 2: Diary of a Prostitute Who Loved Much

1. In most Gentile areas, most Gentile prostitutes were slaves, often abandoned babies that were "rescued" from the trash heaps. They were often employed in taverns. There were also free, high-class prostitutes; they were more "expensive" and fewer men could sleep with them. But this would not be true in Jewish areas.

2. We agree with the countless scholars who believe that the woman in Luke 7 is most likely a prostitute. Although this cannot be proven, it is a highly probable assumption. Women who were called "sinners" in first-century Palestine were typically guilty of some type of sexual offense. (Women couldn't be tax collectors in that day.) This would explain how this woman's notoriety of being a "sinner" was public knowledge.

3. Prostitutes were not only considered impure because of their sexual offenses against the Law and Jewish mores, but because they would fraternize with Gentiles for economic purposes.

4. This is a paraphrase of Ephesians 4:20 KJV.

5. Quoted in Tara Owens, "The Crowd in the Bedroom," http://www.1000strands.com/crowd-in-the-bedroom.

6. Note the many times the Pharisees overtly opposed Jesus. Contrast that with how this sinful woman dared to welcome Him. The faithful disciples love and welcome Jesus, accepting His free offer of grace for them and others.

Chapter 3: Diary of a Desperate Samaritan Woman

1. Samaritans only accepted a revised version of the Pentateuch (the first five books of the Bible) as being sacred. They rejected the rest of Israel's writings. However, they did tell stories and the story of Job could have been one of them. It is for this reason that the Samaritan woman has knowledge of Job's plight in our narrative.

2. Jesus actually used the word "Woman" in the original text. However, in that day, this was not a disrespectful title, but the equivalent of "Ma'am" or "Miss" today. Consequently, we are using "Miss" here to convey what Jesus meant.

3. The Samaritan woman was married five times. Most scholars agree that most—or perhaps all—of these marriages ended in divorce. In the first century, there was no limit to the amount of marriages that could be contracted after a valid divorce. However, the rabbis regarded three marriages to be the maximum for a woman during her lifetime. So this woman's situation was morally untenable.

4. When the Jews wished to be offensive to Jesus, they called him a "Samaritan" (John 8:48). By contrast, Jesus made a Samaritan a hero in one of His parables (Luke 10:25ff.).

5. This was probably traditional custom throughout the eastern Mediterranean, not just in Jewish society.

6. In all existing early Palestinian sources, fewer than 10 percent of women are named. So it wasn't uncommon for the biblical writers to not name the women who appeared in their stories.

7. Isaac (Gen. 24:10ff.); Jacob (Gen. 29:1–20); Moses (Exod. 2:15–21).

8. While Jesus and the Holy Spirit are distinct, they are not separate. Jesus, in His resurrected state, is now in Spirit. So Paul calls the resurrected Christ a "life-giving Spirit" in 1 Corinthians 15:45.

9. *Spoken Word: Woman at the Well* (Jackson: Life Bible Study, 2008), used with permission.

Chapter 4: Diary of a Woman with a Flow of Blood

1. *Zayde* means "grandfather."

2. *Bubbe* means "grandmother."

3. Johnston M. Cheney and Stanley Ellisen, *The Greatest Story Ever Told* (Sisters, OR: Multnomah, 1994), 95–96.

4. Jairus' daughter fell sick and died, but Jesus raised her from the dead.

5. Matthew omits it also. But Matthew omits lots of details because he includes more of Mark's material than Luke does, yet he writes a Gospel of the same length as Luke.

6. While this reference is within the context of believing the gospel message, the principle that faith is built upon hearing God's Word applies to all situations.

7. In Luke 13:16, Jesus refers to a woman as a "daughter of Abraham." But that's not the same as calling someone "Daughter" directly.

8. ESV.

9. See Genesis 32:46.

10. See 2 Corinthians 12:7–10. Of course, if the Lord says to you, "My grace is sufficient," as He told Paul when he asked God to remove his "thorn in the flesh" on three occasions, then you should heed that word. However, if the Lord hasn't said that to you, then press in and don't give up until you receive what you've asked for.

Chapter 5: Diary of the Woman Whom Jesus Loved

1. Psalm 27:13 NLT.

2. Cheney and Ellisen, *Greatest Story Ever Told*, 191–92.

3. Luke 10:39; John 11:32; 12:3.

4. For details supporting and expanding that statement, see Frank Viola, *God's Favorite Place on Earth* (Colorado Springs: David C. Cook, 2013).

5. Ibid., 99–100.

6. ESV.

7. We agree with the countless scholars who show that the banquet mentioned in John, Matthew, and Mark is a different event from the banquet mentioned in Luke 7 where a prostitute anointed the feet of Jesus. The location was different, the characters were different, and the timeline is different.

Chapter 6: One More Thing

1. See Carolyn Custis James, *When Life and Beliefs Collide* (Grand Rapids: Zondervan, 2011).

2. Quoted by John Brown, in *John Bunyan: His Life, Times and Work* (New York: Houghton, Mifflin and Company, 1888), 276.

3. For a detailed look at how the Lord views women, see Frank Viola's blog post, "God's View of a Woman," at http://frankviola.org/view.htm.

Frank Viola has helped thousands of people around the world to deepen their relationship with Jesus Christ and enter into a more vibrant and authentic experience of church. Frank's mission is to help serious followers of Jesus know their Lord more deeply, gain fresh perspectives on old or ignored topics, and make the Bible come alive. He has written many books on these themes, including *God's Favorite Place on Earth* and *From Eternity to Here*. His blog, frankviola.org, is ranked in the top ten of all Christian blogs on the Web today. He lives in Florida and ministers to people all over the world.

Mary DeMuth is a former church planter in France and the author of more than sixteen nonfiction and fiction books. A sought-after speaker and longtime blogger, she has overcome (through Jesus' healing) a difficult childhood full of neglect, abuse, and familial dysfunction to become a living example of what it means to live uncaged. She lives in Texas with her family.

Want to Go Deeper?

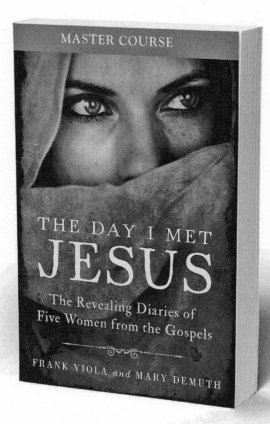

Get THE DAY I MET JESUS Master Course!

The course includes the following:

- Two CDs that contain exclusive audio teachings from Mary and Frank.
- A workbook that provides a "deep dive" into the audio content.
- A special page where you can ask Frank and Mary questions about the content.

Go to TheDayIMetJesus.com for details.

Follow Speaker and Blogger
MARY DeMUTH

Blog: marydemuth.com

facebook.com/AuthorMaryDeMuth

@MaryDeMuth

Follow

FRANK VIOLA

at Beyond Evangelical

Blog: frankviola.org

f facebook.com/frank.viola

🐦 @FrankViola